$24.95

DATE			

Otero Mesa

Rec 1/2/08

1. Flower of a claret cup cactus (*Echinocereus triglochidiatus*). Photograph by Stephen Strom.

OTERO MESA

Preserving America's Wildest Grassland

Text by **Gregory McNamee**

Photographs by **Stephen Strom** and **Stephen Capra**

Foreword by **Governor Bill Richardson**

Additional photographs by **Gregory McNamee**

UNIVERSITY OF NEW MEXICO PRESS ■ ALBUQUERQUE

Printed in Singapore

13 12 11 10 09 08   1 2 3 4 5 6

LIBRARY OF CONGRESS CATALOGING-IN-PUBLICATION DATA

McNamee, Gregory.

Otero Mesa : preserving America's wildest grassland / text by
Gregory McNamee ; photographs by Stephen Strom and Stephen Capra ;
additional photographs by Gregory McNamee.

       p. cm.

ISBN 978-0-8263-4397-0 (pbk. : alk. paper)

1. Grasslands—New Mexico—Otero Mesa.

2. Grassland ecology—New Mexico—Otero Mesa.

3. Grassland conservation—New Mexico—Otero Mesa.

4. Natural history—New Mexico—Otero Mesa.

5. Natural history—New Mexico—Otero Mesa—Pictorial works.

6. Otero Mesa (N.M.) I. Title.

       QH105.N6M36 2008

       333.74'1609789—dc22

          2008007849

Designed and typeset by Mina Yamashita.
Text composed in Utopia Std, a typeface
designed by Robert Slimbach for Adobe in 1989.
Display composed in Frutiger 77 Bold,
designed by Adrian Frutiger in 1976.
Printed by by Tien Wah Press, America on 150gsm Grycksbo Matte.

Contents

List of Illustrations / vi

Foreword by Governor Bill Richardson / ix

Chapter 1

The View from an Aplomado / 1

Chapter 2

The View from a Missile / 27

Chapter 3

Oil / 49

Chapter 4

Otero Mesa and the Fate of the Land / 69

Further Reading / 91

List of Illustrations

1. Flower of a claret cup cactus / ii
2. An aerial view of Otero Mesa / x
3. A summer monsoon storm / xi
4. A winter storm gathers over the San Andres Mountains west of Otero Mesa / xii
5. The Cornudas Mountains / 3
6. A sea of grass flowing / 4
7. An ocotillo / 7
8. Core of a Parry's agave / 9
9. Yellow-headed blackbirds / 11
10. Feather grass in seed / 15
11. Otero Mesa grassland, looking east / 16
12. Otero Mesa grassland, looking west from County Road F37 / 19
13. Flat Top, a peak in the Cornudas Mountains / 20
14. Crossing Otero Mesa at sunset / 24
15. Wind Mountain, a peak in the Cornudas Mountains / 26

16. Grassland and wildflowers in springtime, with the
    Sacramento Mountains in the background / 29
17. Prickly pear cactus / 30
18. Grass in seed, autumn / 35
19. Otero Mesa at sunset / 38
20. A winter storm gathers over the Guadalupe
    Mountains east of Otero Mesa / 43
21. Silverleaf nightshade / 45
22. Otero Mesa grassland under an overcast sky / 46
23. An oil pump at work on the New Mexico plains / 48
24. Oil storage tanks / 51
25. Oil storage tanks and seepage / 56
26. Pronghorn / 59
27. An oil storage tank with a leakage pond / 61
28. A working oil field to the east of Otero Mesa / 66
29. Pepperweed / 68
30. Wildflower mix in springtime / 68
31. The Shiloh Hills, in east-central Otero Mesa / 70

32. The Shiloh Hills near Cornucopia Draw / 71
33. Grass, with the Cornudas Mountains in the
    background / 73
34. Yucca flower / 75
35. Looking south toward Alamo, Wind, and
    Flat Top mountains / 77
36. Pepperweed in springtime / 78
37. A rainbow forms in a summer monsoon storm over
    Otero Mesa / 81
38. Hillsides with ocotillo / 82
39. The Guadalupe Mountains at sunset / 85
40. Grass in seed, fall / 87
41. An immature kestrel / 89

Foreword

Governor Bill Richardson

Since my days in Congress, I have believed that economic growth and environmental protection are not mutually exclusive—that policy makers can produce a win-win situation by striking a reasonable balance between them. New Mexico depends on oil and gas drilling to produce jobs and revenue for the state, and we need to ensure that this important part of the state economy continues to flourish. As I had in Congress, when I entered the statehouse, I told oil and gas people that my door always would be open. But I also said that drilling wasn't an unfettered right, even in a business-friendly administration, and that there were lines I would not cross.

One of them was on Otero Mesa.

Otero Mesa, in the Chihuahuan Desert of south-central New Mexico, features one of the most sweeping areas of native grasslands in North America. Spanning 1.2 million acres, it is environmentally important for several reasons, not least because it carpets a vast groundwater system that should not be exposed to the risks of contamination. It is part of a Global 200 ecoregion designated by the World Wildlife Fund in recognition of its biological diversity. It is also a major source of game important to the state's hunters. It is home to countless species of migratory songbirds, a rare native pronghorn population, prairie dogs, and family-run ranches that in some cases have been in the same family for more than five generations.

From atop Alamo Mountain one can see for scores of miles in any direction. The view is an unbroken sea of grass. At the base of the mountain more than ten thousand petroglyphs are carved

2. An aerial view of Otero Mesa. Photograph by Stephen Capra.

in stone. Such testimony speaks volumes to humankind's history in this harsh and beautiful environment.

For nearly a decade, local oil and gas interests have wanted to open up Otero Mesa to extensive and intrusive oil and gas exploration. In January 2005, thanks to an intensive lobbying effort, the federal Bureau of Land Management approved a plan to drill up to 141 exploratory wells, many of which would fall within the half-million-acre Otero Mesa grasslands. Unchallenged, the likely outcome of this plan will be test wells dotted throughout Otero Mesa, despoiling this pristine and magnificent part of New Mexico.

But a great coalition of hunters, ranchers, religious leaders, businesses, and conservation organizations have made clear their desire to see this area protected. This determination to protect Otero Mesa is not just local, but a national and even international effort.

In 2004 I submitted my own plan for Otero Mesa, which would create a National Conservation Area, zoning off three hundred thousand acres from energy exploration and development and imposing restrictions on the remainder of the land. This plan represents a sensible approach that balances the national need for energy with our commitment to our children and

3. A summer monsoon storm. Photograph by Stephen Capra.

grandchildren to protect our water resources and leave some lands wild and untouched. Yet the Bureau of Land Management said no, and the battle was joined.

As of this writing, the fate of Otero Mesa rests with the courts. However, in the larger sense, preserving places like Otero Mesa will require the engagement of citizens who recognize the value of clean water, open spaces, and the beauty of nature to our own sustenance and that of our descendants.

It is in service to those who must speak for and defend places like Otero Mesa that this book came to be. It tells the story of Otero Mesa—its history, its people, its flora, its fauna, its essential wildness—in both words and images. These often underrepresented elements need to join watershed viability and energy exploration as part of the complex and difficult dialogue that will determine the fate of Otero Mesa and places like it. This dialogue will ultimately lead to priority choices that will affect the environment, the viability of places such as Otero Mesa, and the economy and society that we will leave to future generations. May this book serve to guide wise choices. ◼

4. A winter storm gathers over the San Andres Mountains west of Otero Mesa. Photograph by Gregory McNamee.

Chapter 1

The View from an Aplomado

It is mid-February, and the wind is howling. Through the night, snow has been falling on the Sacramento Mountains, one of the southernmost reaches of the storm-attracting Rocky Mountain cordillera. Now, in early light, great lenticular clouds, looking oddly like flying saucers, have formed high in the eastern sky. Below them, black bands of moisture-laden cumulus snake in and out of the canyons that feed out onto the mountain bajada, spilling water, drop by drop and flake by flake, in the sparing way in which sky feeds an arid country. As it has for millions of years, that water will trickle and tumble down from the Sacramentos, from the Guadalupes, from the Shiloh Hills, and join other water deep below the surface. And there is more water to come, for it is winter, a time of rain and snow, and now thunderheads are forming far down south in Mexico, looming up in the distance a hundred and more miles

away, easily visible from the heights of this broad plateau. Soon enough the thunderheads will arrive, and more water will fall, gathering in the great rocky, grass-covered bowl that is Otero Mesa.

This is a land of sky, a sky so vast and blue that it dwarfs the tallest mountains and broadest valleys. Here it is hard to see not the forest for the trees, but the horizon for the firmament: other places have sky, but here the land seems but a thin strip of dirt under the hugeness of the heavens, that great endless openness punctuated only by clouds. And contrails, of course, for we are in the twenty-first century, so that planes and satellites pass distantly overhead, reminding us of modern realities and appetites that have everything to do with this quiet, distant place.

This is a land of stone, part of a region that geologists call the Trans-Pecos alkaline magmatic province, a thick limestone shelf broken by bursts of lava and long-cooled igneous rock. To the north stand the tall Sacramento Mountains, a great wall of limestone into which water, descending over millions of years, has eroded deep, winding canyons. As the canyons descend to the mesa floor, they continue on as washes and arroyos, such as the nicely named Cornucopia Draw and Rough Draw. To the east loom the Brokeoff Mountains, a spur of the towering Guadalupe Escarpment, which runs down from the Sacramentos to end in the highest peak in Texas, 8,749-foot-tall Guadalupe Peak. Down to the south, curious-looking small peaks rise above Otero Mesa. Among them are Alamo Mountain, which, honoring the Spanish name, sheds water on a small grove of cottonwood trees, and Cornudas Mountain, a heap of broken stones that shelters a kind of land snail that is unique to the place. The tallest of the mountains within the mesa, Wind Mountain, is a long-extinct volcano, its great cone rising to a height of 7,280 feet, lending the landscape an unfinished, primeval look.

A little-visited grassland in southernmost New Mexico, Otero Mesa covers 1.2 million acres, a large area by any standard, even the horizon-stretching standards of the Southwest. It is a strange and empty place, a place whose contours suggest that those who do not know it would do best to leave it alone, as those who do know it will do in all events. And, as with all strange and empty places in this increasingly crowded, increasingly monocultural world, Otero Mesa is an important island in our geography of hope, a place that warrants concern and protection. Rightly, for it is very much under threat.

The Chihuahuan Desert occupies 280,000 square miles, extending 1,200 miles from just north of Otero Mesa all the way down into the Mexican state of Zacatecas. It is the largest desert in North America. Once it was mostly grassland, looking much like Otero Mesa. Today, after a long period of drying beginning in the Pleistocene and

5. The Cornudas Mountains, a weathered volcanic range harboring many kinds of plants and animals. Photograph by Stephen Strom.

6. Grasslands, northwestern quadrant of Otero Mesa. Photograph by Stephen Strom.

rapidly accelerating in these latter days of global warming, it is mostly desert scrubland, with only isolated and generally small stands of grass across most of its extent. The Chihuahuan Desert is not like the comparatively lush Sonoran Desert, where I live; its aridity and great distances can be daunting. The explorer John Russell Bartlett, surveying the country in 1852, voiced just this sentiment in a passage that has become well known to desert rats out this way:

> As we toiled across these sterile plains, where no tree offered its friendly shade, the sun glowing fiercely, and the wind hot from the parched earth, cracking the lips and burning the eyes, the thought would keep suggesting itself, Is this the land which we have purchased, and are to survey and keep at such a cost? As far as the eye can reach stretches one unbroken waste, barren, wild, and worthless.

That view is an old one, a standard in the historical literature, one that just about every non–desert dweller has asked on entering the dry lands. Even old-timers wonder, from time to time, whether the land is not out to get them after all. The novelist Cormac McCarthy, whose Border Trilogy counts Otero Mesa among its settings, has one of his characters looking out on the place and remarking, "No rain. Maybe in the eastern sections. Up in the Sacramentos. People imagined that if you got through a drought you could expect a few good years to try and get caught up but it was just like the seven on a pair of dice. The drought didnt know when the last one was and nobody knew when the next one was coming."

That is just so, even though we know for certain that this is a time of drought, one that shows no signs of ending anytime soon. It is dry country in any case, to be sure. But the Chihuahuan Desert, though surely still wild in many places, is far from barren. In cacti alone it has the greatest diversity of all the North American deserts, though cacti are not among its indicator species —the plants and creatures that indicate, in other words, where in the world you are. Instead, the Chihuahuan Desert's indicators include only one plant that is unique to it, the lechuguilla, a kind of agave, as well as several shrubs found in other deserts, such as the creosote bush, mesquite, and ocotillo.

All of those plants turn up in the desert below Otero Mesa, a low escarpment on the edge of the broad Tularosa Valley. Some of them turn up on the mesa itself; the mesquite, an invader, if less malign than many, has so far kept its distance, but the grassy plain is studded with agaves and ocotillos, reminders, yes, of where we are. The Chihuahuan Desert itself does not extend much farther north of it, only a hundred miles or so, before giving way to other ecosystems. Below the mesa, the Rocky Mountains begin to shade off into the Sierra Madre Oriental, with their great limestone reefs full of caves and hidden lakes, ideal country for bats and mountain lions, rather more

difficult for the farmers and ranchers who, more and more, have been leaving the Mexican countryside for the United States.

A barren place? No, the Chihuahuan Desert, like the Sonoran, is surprisingly diverse, surprisingly generous. And Otero Mesa, a grassland, an ecological island within the surrounding sea of that great desert, is richer still. Its denizens number abundant jackrabbits and cottontails—the former, a hare, common in the lower deserts, the latter, a true rabbit, at home in higher elevations. There are reptiles of all kinds: three kinds of rattlesnakes, rat snakes, king snakes; a dozen species of lizards, including the once plentiful but now declining Texas horned lizard; and turtles and tortoises. There are even four species of toads.

Otero Mesa is home to mule deer and pronghorn, the latter the Formula 1 racer of all North American land mammals, clocking speeds near fifty miles an hour. The mesa's pronghorn population is native to the place, unlike most others in the Southwest,

7. An ocotillo (*Fouquieria splendens*) framed by a setting summer sun. Photograph by Stephen Capra.

reintroduced after having been hunted out early in the twentieth century.

There are peccaries and ringtails, bobcats and elk, mountain lions and coyotes, skunks and foxes, bats and badgers, even a black bear from time to time.

There are black-tailed prairie dogs, who find the hospitality of a natural grassland largely undisturbed by human traffic to be ideally suited to their kind. They take their hibernation seriously, disappearing below ground at the first sign of cold weather and there going about the business of producing the next year's batch of young. In the early spring, when the pups, just weeks old, emerge from underground with their parents, their colonies become antic playgrounds full of little heads popping up everywhere, busily going from mound to mound. Every prairie dog on the mesa has a keen sense of belonging and of social obligation, and thus when trouble comes, as it so often does, one of them will sound an alarm, an unmistakably urgent "chirk-chirk-chirk" sound until all of its fellows are safely underground. When the source of trouble leaves, another prairie dog will sound an all-clear signal, whereupon the prairie dogs celebrate with what biologists call a "jump-yip," which is just that: a vigorous arching of the back, a spring in the air, and a triumphant bark.

They get a lot of practice at all this, for find a prairie dog, and a raptor is likely to be nearby, hoping to find a convenient meal. Fearsome from a small rodent's point of view and impressive by any measure, with their eight-foot wingspans and sharp talons, golden eagles patrol this ground. Joining them are other skilled hunters; in the morning and evening, prime time for chasing game, the sky is alive with bald eagles, prairie falcons, peregrine falcons, kestrels, merlins, and hawks of many kinds, and the ground empty of all but the most incautious mice, gophers, kangaroo rats, squirrels, cottontails, and, of course, prairie dogs.

That the prairie dogs have agreed to cooperate in the face of so much danger is a lesson for us all, I think,

8. Core of a Parry's agave (*Agave parryi*). Photograph by Stephen Strom.

but I have to confess to cheering for another raptor too little seen these days and perfectly at home on Otero Mesa: the aplomado falcon, which ranges as far south as Patagonia and is here at the northern limits of its range. There are not many of these falcons in the world, certainly not north of the Mexico line, perhaps because there are not many wolves in the world either—as the old stories have it, the aplomado spotted prey for the wolf, and the wolf flushed out prey for its helper in thanks.

There are birds: lark buntings, Brewer's sparrows, horned larks, longspurs, black-throated sparrows, yellow-headed blackbirds, more than two hundred species in all. Many of the grasslands species are in a state of slow decline across their range, threatened by habitat fragmentation and outright destruction, what passes for progress in some corners of human society.

There is the bighorn sheep, that characteristic animal of the North American deserts, the only one of the world's major species of sheep not to have contributed to the standard domesticated varieties, being wild at heart and hard to catch. At least, there once was the bighorn sheep. The Sacramentos, the Guadalupes, the Brokeoffs hosted populations in historic times, and scientists are studying Otero Mesa as a reintroduction site, reasoning that the bighorn's former haunt should welcome its return. The highlands suit the bighorns' fondness for rough country, while the lowlands match their apparent pleasure in milking water from stone. That is to say, bighorns do not drink water as such, but rather derive their water from the plant food and dry air of the desert, then filtering the urine through a structure in the kidney—which all mammals have—called the loop of Henle, nature's desalinization plant, so as not to waste a drop of precious water.

There may have been bison out here. We are not sure, but Mescalero Apache sources suggest that their hunters headed onto the mesa to hunt buffalo. The southern herd was exterminated by 1875, and no reliable sources tell us just where the last bison fell. But

9. Yellow-headed blackbirds (*Xanthocephalus xanthocephalus*) gather on a ranch fence. Photograph by Stephen Strom.

the land here is just right for a population of the shaggy beasts, and they certainly would have been better for the land than the bison's successors—for cattle, another Otero Mesa citizen of good standing, blameless creatures though they may be, have the bad habit of standing still for long periods, browsing a patch of grass down to the ground, whereas the great herds of bison that once inhabited the southern plains kept on the move, returning to a given point in the landscape only once every three years or so. They nibbled as they went, and they rarely stayed in one place long enough to leave much of an impression, much less harm it beyond natural recovery.

There is the oryx, a denizen of the African savanna whose history on Otero Mesa is a little fuzzy, even in a part of the country whose history is so often a matter of guesswork. A general at Fort Bliss, the vast army post that extends along the mesa's western boundary, brought in a small herd as a favor to his hunter friends in the 1940s, or so one story has it. Other stories feature different actors, but with the same end: the oryx was originally brought in to be shot for sport, its numbers augmented as the bullets flew. In 1969 the New Mexico Department of Game and Fish brought in several hundred of them elsewhere to swell the state's coffers with fees from lucrative special hunting licenses. In some places, the oryx proved too much of a good thing; in the winter of 1999, for instance, officials at White Sands National Monument launched a program to remove an estimated 140 oryx that had been trapped there when a fence surrounding the monument was completed in 1996. The captive oryx browsed away at the natural vegetation, and they multiplied quite happily, to the point that government officials calculated that were the population left alone, it would grow to thirteen hundred individuals by 2008. They are less abundant on Otero Mesa, because they are hunted quite vigorously, but in their season you can see them racing across the plain, blending in easily with the tawny grasses. Meanwhile, over in central Texas, oryx are becoming a more common sight. Groups working in association with the National Zoo in Washington have brought oryx whose bloodlines had been extirpated in the African wild into places such as the Bamberger Ranch near Austin, while internationally, oryx survival has become a priority for several conservation groups. Otero Mesa's population, it seems, set a good idea in motion.

When I was a child, I once wandered into a swirling dust devil out at White Sands and, enveloped in a white vortex, imagined that I was about to be transported to Oz. The whirlwind did not deliver, but I have had plenty of opportunities to repeat the experiment out here on the mesa, where my father, an army officer, lobbed missiles and artillery shells against a Russian enemy that, so far at least, has not delivered another childhood vision. Otero Mesa is undeveloped, in part, because, far from anything in particular, it lent itself to the requirements of a nation at war, a war that remained cold in name but cost a hundred million

lives all the same. The name of the enemy has changed since, and Otero Mesa may not outlast the new war, but it bears considering that its peace may owe in some measure to conflict, and that good things are worth fighting for.

The peace-in-war turn would not be the first of the ironies to visit the great American desert, not by a long shot. For the moment, I set aside that thought, for the cold wind is blowing ever harder, as it always does on Otero Mesa, and I am looking deeply into the quizzical eyes of a Black Angus. A small herd of them has gathered, blocking the path in what passes for bovine defiance, letting me know that I am the stranger here, and that this is their domain. It is a point I am not inclined to protest, even if I'm secretly rooting for the bison.

This is a place of stone, of tall agaves, of constant wind. A place where water falls sparingly from the sky and where stone shepherds that scant water into deep hiding places. But this is preeminently a place of grass:

black grama, blue grama, sideoats grama, sacaton, bristlegrass, purple threeawn, tobosagrass, cane bluestem, bush muhly—thirteen species in all, making a cover that is lush and densely woven compared to other desert grasslands. This particular grassland in the desert is one of the rarest of all North American ecosystems: an island of waving grain in an advancing sea of brown, the last of its kind.

Grasslands are essential to the health of the world, far more than just the earth's shaggy golden mane. They have been essential to humankind, too, sowing the civilizations that, in the words of that great grasslands ballad "John Barleycorn," have treated them most barbarously ever since.

Thousands of years ago, by some cosmic intuition that modern historians have yet to explain, nomadic peoples around the world came to understand that they could extract a basic diet from the grasses around them. In East Asia, that grass was rice. In Eurasia, it was wheat. In North America, it was corn. All three were domesticated at roughly the same time; all three provided the agricultural basis for the urban civilizations that would soon rise around fertile grain fields and paddies; all three became staples of the world, spread far beyond their original homelands.

Ten-thousand-odd years ago, in the horseshoe-shaped highlands of what are now Iraq, Turkey, Syria, and Israel, places that look very much like Otero Mesa, Stone Age hunter-gatherers made a fateful discovery: a grass that grew on the mountain slopes grew particularly large seeds that, with some work, could be removed and eaten. What was more, this grass, called einkorn, a variety of wild wheat, yielded easily to cutting with flint blades. Forty years ago, archaeologist Jack Harlan determined that, working with a flint sickle, he alone was capable of harvesting more than two pounds of clean grain every hour, and of a much higher concentration of proteins than the winter wheat grown on the plains of North America now produces. The work would have required no permanent

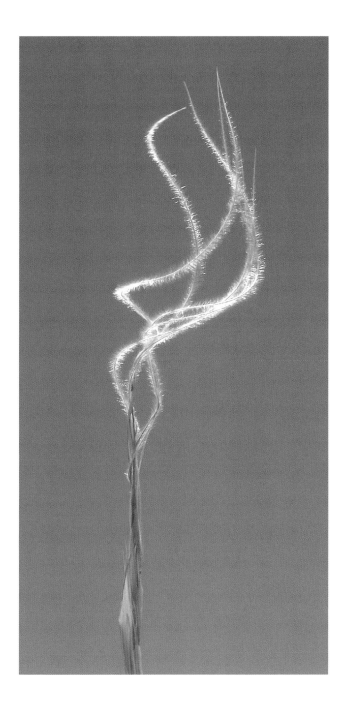

10. Feather grass in seed.
Photographs by Stephen Strom.

11. Otero Mesa grassland, looking east. Photograph by Stephen Strom.

settlements; a Neolithic family resident in that so-called Fertile Crescent could have traveled into the mountains seasonally and, in the space of weeks, gathered enough einkorn grain to feed themselves for a year and even enjoy some surplus.

Thus the seeds of capitalism. Permanent settlements followed nonetheless, and, beginning in about 7500 BC, the hill country began to sprout sturdy little towns such as Jericho, Beidha, Çatalhöyük, and Tell Hassuna. Thus the seeds of Western civilization—which may have resulted, geographer Jonathan Sauer speculated in the 1950s, not from the production of bread as a foodstuff per se but of beer. Whatever the case, within a few generations of settling down into towns, these now-committed farming people made further discoveries, among them the fact that einkorn and emmer could be modified and improved to reduce the curious habit of these grains' spikes shattering as soon as they were ripe, which allowed the wild grains to seed themselves more readily. By gaining at least some measure of control over this shattering, the farmers could transport cultivable grains beyond the mountains, and soon wheat was everywhere in the ancient world.

We cannot say with any confidence when humans

hit on the idea of domesticating the bright green grass that grew wild below the southeastern foothills of the Himalaya Mountains, a grass that spread from there across southern Asia deep in antiquity and that now serves as the single most important foodstuff for fully half of humanity: rice. A set of pottery jars unearthed in the Neolithic village of Jiahu, in northern China's Henan Province, contains the earliest evidence of rice cultivation that we have, which lends itself to Sauer's hypothesis, for within them was a mixed fermented beverage of rice, honey, and fruit dating to at least 7000 BC. Whatever the case, at least one hundred thousand varieties of rice, about 8 percent of which have been thoroughly domesticated, have been grown since.

First domesticated in the Valley of Mexico, *Zea mays* originated from *Zea mexicana*, a wild grass commonly called teosinte. This floury-kerneled maize required a growing period of only ninety to one hundred days (varieties grown today mature in anywhere from sixty to three hundred days), making it a relatively quick source of nourishment. Its adaptation also allowed the native peoples of Mexico—and, thanks to its rapid spread across the two continents, indigenous cultures elsewhere in the Americas—to escape the cycles of feast and famine that had governed their lives. A hardy, low-maintenance plant, maize also allowed its first cultivators to do other things than chase up food—that is, to build pyramids, ballcourts, palaces, and empires. The last, arguably, owe directly to corn, for among the greatest innovations in world military technology, the Mesoamerican prehistorian Ross Hassig argues, was the tortilla, the thin, dried corn cake that graces tables in Mexican restaurants around the world. So commonplace an item that we scarcely give it a thought today, the tortilla, Hassig has demonstrated, was developed so that Aztec armies on the march could have a quick source of nourishment, a kind of New World proto–C ration. It enabled Aztec troops to travel quickly through much of Mexico, bringing the light of their civilization to their usually unwilling neighbors at the obsidian point of a spear.

Christopher Columbus, a military-minded man, probably never saw the tortilla in action. He nonetheless brought back an abundance of corn to Spain from his first voyage to the Caribbean, ranging from dwarf varieties to giant strains that grew eighteen feet high. Some of these varieties flourished in Spain, but most others did not. Those varieties that survived were soon exported across the world, and corn (known as maize in all English-speaking countries save for the United States and Canada) has become a staple foodstuff in places as far afield as the Philippines, Romania, and Senegal.

We owe our world to grasses. We owe much of what we eat to grasses, including several that grow natively on Otero Mesa. It stands to reason that we ought to treat the grasses and the grasslands with more respect. But then, as the story of Otero Mesa tells us, we ought to treat the world with more respect—or at least fight harder to protect it from its enemies.

Look at a physical map of the world. Follow the tropics of Cancer and Capricorn, thirty degrees on either side of the equator, and you will see a brown band of deserts circling the planet. They lie in the horse latitudes, where constant high-pressure systems separate the westerly and trade winds, driving away the rain clouds. Some of those dry lands, such as the Atacama of Chile, the Namib and Kalahari deserts of southern Africa, and the western Australian desert, are the result of cold ocean currents that divert rain-laden air away from coastlines. Others, such as the Gobi and Taklimakan deserts of Mongolia and China, are so far away from the ocean that the winds lose any moisture they may hold long before reaching the faraway continental interior. Still others, such as the Chihuahuan Desert and the deserts of central and eastern Australia, are caused by the rain shadow effect, through which coastal mountains milk rain from the air before it passes inland.

The world's desert systems are harsh environments: by definition, a desert receives less than ten inches of

12. Otero Mesa grassland, looking west from County Road F37. Photograph by Stephen Strom.

unevenly distributed rain throughout the year, though it need not suffer extreme heat. (Antarctica, for example, is a desert where rain never falls and no vegetation grows and where it is seldom warm.) Those deserts now cover more than 20 percent of the planet's surface, a figure that grows substantially each year thanks to the phenomenon of desertification, a process of soil erosion and land degradation that occurs when land that normally receives little rain is stripped of whatever vegetation it has.

Desertification can result from several more or less natural processes that are harmless enough one by one but can play ecological havoc in combination. One is the ongoing process of global warming, which is altering weather patterns around the world, bringing drought to once temperate zones. Another is the desiccating El Niño weather system in the Pacific, which has been prevalent for much of the past decade and which has led to a virtual end of summer rain in the deserts of North and South America.

But the most powerful agent of desertification is humankind. With the growing world population, formerly marginal areas on the fringes of deserts are becoming more heavily settled. With humans come

13. Flat Top, a peak in the Cornudas Mountains. Photograph by Stephen Capra.

livestock, which devour the already scant ground vegetation; taller trees and shrubs are cleared away for fuelwood. The removal of plant life means that when rain falls, it cannot penetrate the dry soil, once broken by plant roots; instead, it runs off the surface toward low ground in a process that hydrologists call "sheet flooding." In the last quarter century, according to United Nations statistics, at least 128,000 people have died as a result of such floods.

Desertification has caused tremendous social change in affected areas, especially in sub-Saharan Africa and Central America, where famine is now a constant danger and where massive flooding and mudslides follow even modest rainfall. In these areas, desertification has caused the destruction of rural agriculture and a massive migration of country people into already crowded cities; in 2000 there were more than twenty-five million such "environmental refugees," a far greater number than those fleeing war or political oppression. Some fifty million more,

the United Nations estimates, will join their number in the next decade.

Desertification has emerged as a major environmental problem in some unlikely areas, and not in the Third World alone. In the deserts of the United States, areas that have been intensively grazed and farmed have grown a thick skin of salts and other minerals, making the land useless for further agriculture. In Beijing, dust storms from the nearby Gobi are a regular hazard, while the Gobi's sand dunes advance toward the city at a rate of fifteen miles a year—and are now just sixty miles away. In Italy, Spain, and elsewhere in the Mediterranean, intensive olive farming has led to soil erosion and canyon-cutting, and great areas of land are now unsuitable for agriculture.

Desertification is not unstoppable, but containing its spread will require massive international efforts and cost trillions of dollars. Any measures to halt its growth will involve continued economic hardship for the people most affected by desertification, for they include putting an end to livestock grazing and irrigated agriculture until plant cover has returned to a denuded stretch of ground, a process that can take decades. International aid organizations are working to convert farmers and herders in places like the Sahel and northwestern India into modern-day Johnny Appleseeds, planting hedgerows and windbreaks to halt the advancing sands. The fate of hundreds of millions of lives and of millions of acres hinges on their success or failure.

Otero Mesa is a seawall against an advancing desert. Without protection, without constant vigilance, it too, will disappear.

A theoretical study conducted at Ben-Gurion University of the Negev, in Israel, shows how deserts grow out of grasslands. A grassland, technically called a semiarid plant vista, develops the equivalent of bald spots as aridity increases—as it surely is, in the Chihuahuan Desert and elsewhere in the world.

These bald spots expand to form banded, labyrinthine clusters of plants whose hold on the soil becomes ever more tenuous. Under a healthy grasslands regime, such as now obtains on Otero Mesa, perennial plants with well-developed root systems capture water efficiently, even under arid conditions. When even a portion of that cover is removed, then a bald spot can quickly become a bald plain.

One way to kill a grassland, in North America, is to kill its prairie dogs, which protect it in several ways. For one thing, their tunnels aerate the soil, allowing rainwater to penetrate more readily to a plant's roots. For another, a prairie dog enjoys few things more than eating the shoots of young shrubs such as mesquite, a plant that plays an accessory role in turning grasslands into deserts. The prairie dogs' colonies, thirty-two of which grace Otero Mesa, provide a roof for many animals—not only the prairie dogs themselves, but also spiders, burrowing owls, rattlesnakes, salamanders, turtles, skunks, badgers, and other species that have adapted to heat by finding cool comfort underground. Whether because they give aid and comfort to these creepy-crawlies or because the holes were dangerous traps for unobservant cattle, and therefore inimical to the ranching economy, a century ago the federal government initiated a widespread campaign to eradicate prairie dogs, setting strychnine bait and other death-dealing mechanisms for them, and thus became one agent for the desert's advance.

If they are to retain their vigor, grasslands have to be disturbed from time to time. One disturbance is to be trod upon by bison and other large browsers. Another disturbance is flooding. Hailstorms and frosts do their work, as do tornadoes. But the most effective disturbance, supplied by nature every ten or fifteen years, is a good grass fire, one that takes the grass down to the ground and supplies nitrogen and other nutrients to the soil. The grass will come back, lushly, but other vegetation will not, most important among it invading shrubs. Fires, like prairie dogs, keep shrubs in check: they keep grasslands from becoming forests, from becoming deserts.

A combination of overgrazing, the destruction of prairie dog colonies, fire suppression, drought, and climate change has severely diminished the number, extent, and quality of Chihuahuan Desert grasslands in the last century. They have made an orphan of Otero Mesa north of the Mexican border. And there are other ways to kill a grassland that are under consideration for the place, ways that involve disturbance taken to extremes: the digging of roads and oil-well pads, the fragmentation of habitat, the disruption of migration routes for birds and mammals, the annihilation of old ways of life.

To arrive at Otero Mesa, you must travel a good distance, and that is just as it should be. Missiles and shells may fly overhead from time to time, and that is all to the good. Once you have arrived, the wind will try to pick you up and carry you away, and that is one more

14. Crossing Otero Mesa at sunset. Photograph by Stephen Capra.

sign that at least something is right with the world.

The nearest cities, Alamogordo, New Mexico, and El Paso, Texas, are an hour and more away. There are only a few ways to get there, short of walking. One is to brave the Sacramentos and their vertiginous canyons and drop down through the pines and serrated hills onto the northern edge of the mesa. Another is to come up through the rutted, abraded, salty Texas desert from Dell City or by way of ranch roads farther west, climbing slowly up the bajada of the Cornudas Mountains. Still another is to ascend from the one vantage where it becomes immediately evident why Otero Mesa deserves its name: the western approach from the highway that joins El Paso and Alamogordo, and from there travels all the way to Canada, picking your way over the artillery range as a low but still quite evident escarpment comes ever closer into view, rising to the great enclosed watershed that lies beyond.

However you come, over one bumpy dirt road or another, you will arrive in a world of waving grasses, golden, brown, and green in their seasons. You will come to country where the views extend for scores of miles in every direction. You will arrive in a place that has largely been left to do what it is supposed to do, which is to be that grassy remoteness. You will come to that rarest of places, a habitat that is whole, not carved up into the bite-sized pieces favored by an always hungry economic machine.

You will arrive at a place that needs more guardians. The aplomado falcon flying overhead, watching your movements, is a very good start, but Otero Mesa needs us as well. ▪

15. Otero Mesa, late afternoon. Photograph by Stephen Strom.

Chapter 2

The View from a Missile

Otero Mesa is a quiet place. Otero Mesa, it would seem, has always been a quiet place, inhabited in the very distant past by migrant Paleo-Indians whose culture a standard archaeological reference terms "poorly known archaic." Those hunters, who arrived in the region some twelve thousand years ago and perhaps earlier, would have found a much different landscape from that of today: a grassland still, but much more thoroughly watered, for the annual rainfall then was something more than forty inches, about the level Iowa now receives. Active glaciers gnawed through the highlands, while down on the valley floors a strange menagerie roamed.

Archaeologist Richard MacNeish, whose work has been important in understanding the agricultural pre-history of North America, excavated two cave sites on the McGregor Firing Range, a part of the vast Fort Bliss military reservation bordering Otero Mesa, and found the flint-butchered bones of *Equus niobrensis*, a large horse prevalent on the Great Plains until about thirty thousand years ago—flint-butchered requiring human contact and long before the standard chronology says that humans arrived here. Other bones, identified as the long-extinct Aztlan rabbit and extinct miniature *Eohippus*, or "dawn horse," found in association with human remains push the dates of occupation back to at least forty thousand years before the present.

Archaeologists will have to hash out an accepted chronology, but for the moment the evidence suggests that Otero Mesa was a fine larder, offering mastodons and Columbian mammoths, elephantine creatures that were the largest terrestrial species on the North American continent, as well as tapirs, sloths, the dire wolf, the four-pronged antelope, and—what surely must have impressed the Paleo-Indian hunters who encountered it—a giant bear that stood ten feet tall at the shoulder. The early hunters would have gone after other animals as well, some of them now extinct: prairie dogs, camels, tapirs, short-faced bears, tigers, deer, badgers, wolves, jaguars, horses, and bison.

The climate changed, as climate will, and, in combination with the zeal of the hunters, over time these abundant animals began to disappear. The mesa's tobosagrass and black grama grasses would feed the last of the bison in the Southwest, and then there were no more bison either. The face of the region began to change, taking on familiar contours: dry grasslands now, punctuated by sand dunes and other desert features, studded by agaves and cacti.

The mountains, now without their glaciers, offered better pickings, and bands of Paleo-Indians began to settle in country that previously had been too cold for them. In the Mogollon Mountains at the headwaters of the Gila River, about two hundred miles west of

Otero Mesa, they acquired from itinerant traders from central Mexico seeds cultivated from *Zea mexicana*, or teosinte, that immeasurably important grass transformed into *Zea mays* and its kin: maize. The floury-kerneled native corn required a growing period of only ninety to a hundred days, and its adaptation allowed the people of the Southwest to escape cycles of feast and famine, giving rise to sedentary agriculturalism in the highlands of the Sacramento Mountains and elsewhere in what is now New Mexico.

The result, we can conjecture, is that the mesa lands became quieter still, people passing through only to gather food plants in season and to hunt. The highlands themselves were probably well populated, however, and if you toe up an inch or two of dirt near where the mesa meets the mountains, you'll likely find bits and pieces of pottery and bone and the occasional flaked point to testify to the presence of the ancestors, to say nothing of the abundant "pictographs upon the rimland boulders that bore images of hunter

16. Grassland and wildflowers in springtime, with the Sacramento Mountains in the background. Photograph by Stephen Strom.

and shaman and meetingfires and desert sheep all beneath a band of dancers holding hands like paper figures scissored out by children and stenciled on the stone," as Cormac McCarthy writes in *Cities of the Plain* (1998)—a book that divides its time between quiet Otero Mesa and the noisy cities of El Paso, Ciudad Juárez, and faraway Phoenix.

A few centuries before Columbus's arrival, in another disputed chronology, a new group of hunters arrived in Otero Mesa from the distant north. They were the Mescaleros, who ranged between the Sacramento Mountains and the plains to the south and east,

going down to the mesa to gather the agaves that gave them their name.

Out on the mesas, one Mescalero recalled centuries after his people's arrival, they found all they needed: not only the agaves, but also cottontails and prairie dogs, gophers and bighorn sheep, porcupines and even the occasional bear. He killed a silver-tip, the man told anthropologist Morris Opler, in the foothills of the Sacramento Mountains above the mesa, adding, "A general at Fort Bliss got that hide from me. He carries it still."

An Apache-speaking group with a territory that extended far south into Mexico, the Mescaleros kept on

17. Prickly pear cactus (*Opuntia phaeacantha*) flowers (detail). Photograph by Stephen Strom.

the move, traveling in season between the cold twelve-thousand-foot-tall mountains and the hot, dry valleys, preferring a gathering and hunting regime to the extensive farming of their Puebloan neighbors along the Rio Grande, but also, like other Apaches, practicing a form of esteem-building that involved raiding those neighbors and anyone else who might happen along. Apache raiding, as scholars have pointed out, was rarely wanton and seldom involved killing; the point was to steal away as many animals or perhaps trade goods or, less often, children as possible without incurring death oneself or inflicting it on others. It was a profitable enterprise with

the added benefit of counting coup, in other words, with an etiquette evolved over the centuries, and everyone in Native America seems to have understood the rules, even if the raided would in time come to exact all manner of revenge on the raiders.

Early in March 1536, four men, dressed in tattered animal skins, came to the gates of a ranch in Sonora. They were questioned and fed, then taken to the city of Culiacán, where their forty-four-year-old leader told a fantastic story. His name was Álvar Núñez Cabeza de Vaca, he said. He and two soldiers, along with a freed slave called Estevanico, had walked from the coast of Texas, where they had been shipwrecked eight years earlier as members of the unfortunate Narváez expedition. There were three hundred of them when they started, and now there were just the four.

They saw and did miraculous things, Cabeza de Vaca averred. They had raised Indians from the grave, had cured blindness, had been hailed as gods and were given, he recounted, "beads made of coral from the South Sea, fine turquoises from the north—in fact, everything the Indians had, including a fine gift to me of five emerald arrowheads." Cabeza de Vaca could not produce any of these treasures, and soon he would be accused of sorcery and bound to Spain for trial, but his listeners paid attention when he said that the Indians to the north had pointed the direction toward seven fabulous adjoining cities made entirely of gold. Their name, he said, was Cíbola.

Three years later, Francisco Vásquez de Coronado, the governor of the province of Nueva Galicia,

dispatched Estevanico and Friar Marcos de Niza to locate the cities of gold. De Niza returned several months later with mixed reports: they had found the cities of gold, he said, but hostile Indians had murdered Estevanico.

De Niza sketched out a map taking in thousands of miles of territory, recounting, like Cabeza de Vaca, great mountains and rivers, vast plains, and uncounted riches. Rodrigo de Albornoz, the royal treasurer of New Spain, summarized de Niza's report:

> There are seven very populous cities with great buildings. . . . The name of one where he has been is Cíbola, the others are in the Kingdom of Marata. There is very good news of other very populous countries, of their riches and good order and manner of living, also of their edifices and other things. They have houses built of stone and lime, being of three stories, and with great quantities of turquoise embedded

in the doors and windows. Of animals there are camels and elephants and cattle . . . and a great number of sheep like those of Peru, also other animals with a single horn reaching to the ground, for which reason they must feed sideways. These are not unicorns but some other kind of creature. The people are said to go clothed to the neck, like Moors. They are known to be people of solid understanding.

There was almost nothing truthful in what Albornoz so diligently recorded, though it is tempting to think that the "other kind of creature" was the bison. In any event, on February 22, 1540, Coronado set out with three hundred Spanish soldiers and a thousand Indian bearers. They trudged across rough mountain country that left his men and animals exhausted, but when they left the mountains, he recalled, "we found fresh rivers and grass like that of Castile." The country, Coronado reported, was *despoblado*, "uninhabited," perhaps because of his vanguard—epidemic disease, which had probably come into the country a dozen years before any actual conquistador did, laying pueblos and *rancherías* low with smallpox, measles, influenza, typhus, pertussis, bubonic plague, tuberculosis, diphtheria, mumps, and yellow fever.

Following de Niza's map, Coronado and his soldiers continued onward until they encountered a dusty village called Shiwona, or Zuni, a word Spanish ears heard as "Cíbola." It was not made of gold, Coronado discovered, prompting him to write a letter to the ruler of New Spain, Viceroy Mendoza, charging that Friar de Niza had "not told the truth in a single thing he has said, for everything is the very opposite of what he related except the name of the cities." Wounded in the siege of Zuni, Coronado took months to recover, then moved down the Rio Grande to the vicinity of what is now El Paso, where a Tigua Indian told him of a great city far to the east called Quivira, which Coronado again heard as "Cíbola."

The expedition turned east and out on a vast plain a couple of days' ride away encountered so many bison that the soldier who chronicled the journey "did not know what to compare them with except the fish in the sea." This place may have been Otero Mesa, though that chronicle is so approximate that we can only guess at the itinerary, which lasted two years and took the force to northeastern Kansas before Coronado took a bad fall from a horse and turned his men—now a mere handful, like Cabeza de Vaca's group—back to Mexico, where Coronado died, broken, at the age of forty-four.

Over the next half century Otero Mesa was the province of Mescaleros and other Apaches, with perhaps a few wide-ranging Comanches thrown into the mix. Then, in 1598, provincial governor Juan de Oñate drove herds of cattle and sheep into what is now southern New Mexico east and west of the Rio Grande, finding savannas where the native grasses, he reported, stood as high as a man on horseback. Soon small ranches sprang up, largely staffed by Pueblo Indians from northern New Mexico, who suffered Apache raids prompted by the sudden riches that lay before the raiders. Don Juan Ignacio Flores de Mogollón, for whom the Mogollon Rim is named, campaigned against the Apaches in the west, while an Indian fighter named Juan Domínguez de Mendoza later turned Spain's attention to the Mescaleros.

In 1692 open war broke out, fueled in part by the Mescaleros' support for the Pueblo Revolt a dozen years earlier, the governing idea doubtless being of the enemy-of-my-enemy-is-my-friend sort. In one episode, Governor Antonio de Otermín sent a powerful force high into the stronghold of the Organ Mountains and drove the Mescaleros eastward onto Otero Mesa, but the Indians eluded the Spaniards' grasp and harried other expeditions throughout the 1690s, even raiding El Paso for horses and cattle.

Conditions did not improve over the next two centuries, and Mescalero raids on Spanish settlements continued. They had two effects: they kept the mesa country largely empty of settlers, and they kept the Mescaleros apart from certain material advantages that the Pueblos enjoyed, not least a year-round supply of food. Hugo O'Conor was the most successful of the European soldiers to go up against the Mescaleros, and he came to appreciate the vastness of their territory and, good guerrilla fighter that he had been, the safety it afforded his foe. But in the end the Irish nobleman went westward to found the presidio of Tucson for the Spanish crown, leaving the war to the French-born Teodoro de Croix, who recruited Lipan Apaches to fight the Mescaleros (and, from time to time, Mescaleros to fight the Lipan) and in time convinced some of the Mescaleros to settle at the junction of the Conchos River and the Rio Grande—a place, Spanish authorities soon realized, that became a staging point for Apache raids deep into Mexico. Finally, Mexican authorities offered a treaty eleven years after their nation's independence from Spain, and the Mescaleros were largely left to their former vast territories with the understanding that they would in turn leave Mexico be.

The treaty did not last, especially not after certain Mescaleros joined in the fight for Texas independence. Like so many native peoples of the Southwest, at first they regarded the arriving Americans as liberators against the much-hated Spanish, who were in the habit of offering bounties for Indian dead, introducing a novel method of taking body counts: for every ear brought in they paid twenty pesos, for every scalp fifty. (There was no way to determine, of course, whether these were truly of Mescalero provenance.) By 1800, when the route south from Santa Fe and from the newly discovered Santa Rita copper mines at the headwaters of the Gila River fell under constant attack from Apaches of all kinds, the rate increased to a hundred pesos for each head of enemy hair, and soon a mat of scalps numbering in the thousands bedecked the great doors of the cathedral in Chihuahua City.

18. Grass in seed, autumn. Photograph by Stephen Strom.

The Mescaleros would soon discover that the Americans had other interests in mind than treating Indian rights squarely. An early encounter came in 1835, when James Johnson, an American trader, cut a swath of death through the countryside before arriving at Santa Rita del Cobre to call a conference with an Apache war leader named Juan José. Johnson, representing the governor of Chihuahua, who had charged him with settling the Apache problem in any manner he chose, told Juan José that he had brought a sack of flour for the women and children, who gathered around it eagerly. One of Johnson's men then fired a six-pound cannon that had been hidden under a mule blanket, its barrel filled with nails, musket balls, glass, and bits of chain. Twenty Apache women died, dozens more Apaches were maimed, and an untold number of others died also, Juan José among them. One of the American participants would go on to become the first American mayor of Los Angeles, where Johnson would move and live out a long and prosperous life.

American cattle soon took the place of Spanish and Mexican cattle out on the mesa, guarded by watchful vaqueros and local regulators who were sometimes given to fighting among themselves when other targets were not available. One bit of divisive politics involved the vast salt deposits within sight of Otero Mesa, below Guadalupe Peak, to which a Republican politician and prominent attorney named Albert J. Fountain held provisional title, along with partner W. W. Mills. In 1872 a former Confederate officer and attorney named Charles Howard filed claim on the salt lakes, whereupon another Democratic politician, Louis Cardis, powerful among the Hispanic community, protested that the salt was in the public domain, and the parties argued in and out of court for the next few years while crowds of supporters battled out on the range. In 1877 Howard killed Cardis and was in time arrested by forerunners of the Texas Rangers. An armed contingent of Cardis's supporters besieged the post where Howard was being kept and executed Howard, turning the rangers out. The rangers soon returned with the army in tow, and Cardis's champions slipped away into Mexico. Thus ended the El Paso Salt War, which had one lasting effect: Fort Bliss, the U.S. Army outpost, had been abandoned at the close of the Civil War, but now it was commissioned anew and extended to include a vast domain that would one day border Otero Mesa itself.

By 1872 the Mescaleros had been pushed up into the mountains, where, they protested, the game was limited and the weather often severe, and where no agaves grew. Once the Mescaleros were off the land, it became the province of large ranches owned, sometimes in absentia, by the likes of Albert Fall, who would later be implicated in the Teapot Dome oil scandal of the 1920s, and Oliver Lee, a cattleman who arrived from Texas in 1892 and carved out a vast empire that, locals whispered, was built on cattle that bore brands other than his. Lee had a way of dispatching enemies who whispered loudly enough; among other crimes,

he was implicated in 1896 in the murder of Fountain, who had moved to New Mexico after the Salt War, and Fountain's young son. The charge was never proved, for the bodies were never found, despite the best efforts of the local sheriff, Pat Garrett—the killer of Billy the Kid, that frequent haunter of Otero Mesa. It did not hurt Lee's case that Fall, a prominent attorney on his way to becoming a Republican senator and Washington powerbroker, defended him, charging that Lee's accusers were engaged in "a conspiracy to send an innocent man to the gallows."

Lee has a park named for him just outside of Alamogordo, while Fall figures, usually poorly, in the history books. Few other ranchers out on Otero Mesa enjoyed renown beyond the mesa itself, which returned to its former quiet for decades—a peace that would be broken by a new kind of landlord.

In the predawn morning of July 16, 1945, a half-mile-long freight train labored up a winding grade between

19. Otero Mesa at sunset. Photograph by Stephen Capra.

Deming and Las Cruces, New Mexico. As the train topped a tall hill, a flash of light burst high above the eastern horizon, widening and deepening against the blackness of the sky, spreading in all directions, roaring. The light hung in the air for a few seconds, then faded away, leaving on the clouds an eerie imprint.

At first the train's conductor thought that the blazing light was heat lightning. But the winds blew from the wrong direction, and the steadiness of the fire did not match the impetuous here-and-there nature of a desert electrical storm. He then thought, for a panicked moment, that the light might have been artillery fire aimed at Japanese aircraft, for, rumor had it, the Japanese were about to mount a last-ditch, desperate invasion from nearby Mexico.

In the rail yard at Las Cruces the conductor compared his impressions with those of other workers. None of them had a ready explanation for what they had seen. After a few beers and some talk back and forth, they decided it must have been lightning after all, if lightning of a ferocity none of them had seen before.

Standing in his front yard in downtown Tucson half a century later, the conductor, my next-door neighbor for fifteen years, said quietly, "It wasn't but a few weeks later that we dropped the A-bombs on the Japs. That's when we figured out that what we saw was some kind of test." He paused for a moment, remembering. "I can still see it all these years later, that light in the sky."

The Trinity atomic bomb test, which the conductor had witnessed that night, was one of many experiments government scientists had been conducting in southern New Mexico. Most of those tests were not nearly so visible, kept as closely guarded secrets. In one, scientists working for the U.S. Army Air Corps attempted to develop a weapon employing hundreds of incendiary charge–laden Mexican freetail bats. When released in midair, these bats, the scientists hoped, would take refuge in the rafters and rooftops of Japan's major cities and, when ignited by delayed fuses, would set off a huge firestorm to visit an inferno on the enemy. The experiment was short-lived; the bats instead burned down the laboratory that held them.

Trinity was of an altogether different magnitude, and it would change history. With it, death left the

battlefield and traveled freely everywhere. As former president Herbert Hoover remarked just a few months after the test, "Despite any sophistries, we have introduced to the world a weapon whose only conceivable purpose is to kill women, children, and civilian men of whole cities."

From the waterless atomic desert of Hiroshima and Nagasaki to the nuclear desert of America is a short step. Far though it lies from the Fulda Gap and the 38th parallel, the American West took its place as the chief arena in which the Cold War was waged at home. Today, something like the equivalent of a million Nagasaki-size warheads lie in atomic embryo throughout the region, squirreled away for another time. The war made a proving ground of the Western desert, a laboratory for subterranean thermonuclear explosions, even as Russia and China tested their thermonuclear arsenals in their own deserts and Britain visited its fledgling nuclear might on the deserts of Australia.

As a downwinder, a resident of the Southwest

during much of the period when those tests were being conducted, I long ago came to take the atomic issue personally. Born in 1957, the year of Sputnik, I grew up with the Bomb. I was born a dozen years after the dawn of the atomic age, just at the start of the space race, two years after Disneyland opened, three years before Sun City beckoned its first retirees. As a child, I lived on military bases, and I suppose I thought that every normal backyard in America opened onto a view that featured a missile or two, as mine always did. My father was an artillery officer, testing rockets at White Sands and on the McGregor Range, bordering the western edge of Otero Mesa. He served two tours of duty in Vietnam, did time at the Pentagon. For my part, I marched in antiwar demonstrations and wrote for underground newspapers, praying that my turn at the front would not come.

My story is by no means unusual; the experiences of millions of Americans intersect with one or another of its main points. I raise it only because I want to emphasize how the Cold War, with its one hundred million dead around the world, defined the culture in which I came of age and grew well into adulthood, and which, I believe, continues to define the attitude of the state—the state writ large, that is—with respect to the supposedly empty, supposedly remote lands of the desert West, lands that lend themselves easily only to the work of serving as national sacrifice areas.

That culture was in turn defined by cartoons and symbols and shorthand, by the pointless exercise of clambering under wooden hingetop desks for protection from a thermonuclear blast, as if that would help. "Don't get excited or excite others," Bert the Turtle, the icon of civil defense, instructed us. We did not, as children, disobey him, although nuclear dreams troubled our sleep and nuclear realities brought us endless disappointments. Weaving the Cold War and the Bomb into our odd private mythology, we watched the movies—*Attack of the 50 Foot Woman*, *Night of the Lepus*, *Tarantula*—and watched the skies, and we waited.

Indeed, if the geography of the movie *Them* is to be trusted, giant atomic-mutant ants marched straight across Otero Mesa on their way to pulverize Los Angeles, which turns out to be not such a bad idea.

The bomb, the culture of the bomb, deprived me and my age-mates of a vision of the future, at least for many years. Instead, we had commodity capitalism, production as destruction, an intolerable work world of lies and waste. And what waste it was. The Czech energy economist Vaclav Smil observes that the development of nuclear weapons has consumed a tenth of the energy used worldwide since 1945—which has much bearing on our immediate subject, as we will see in the following chapter.

Ours was a generation looted of its patrimony, as Dwight Eisenhower said in a famous speech of April 16, 1953:

> Every gun that is made, every warship launched, every rocket fired signifies in the final sense a theft from those who hunger and are not fed, those who are cold and are not clothed. The world in arms is not spending money alone. It is spending the sweat of its laborers, the genius of its scientists, the hopes of its children. This is not a way of life at all in any true sense. Under the clouds of war, it is humanity hanging on a cross of iron.

We hung there on that cross for the duration of our youth, certain that we had no future. We comforted ourselves with nihilism, with the easiness of seize-the-day philosophies and other spiritual black holes, while our elders proved to us that our hopelessness was well grounded. All we needed for proof was the folly of Star Wars, another bit of mass-produced symbolism overlaid on the face of horror, born in the Reagan years and reborn in the Age of Bush II.

The cities to which Herbert Hoover adverted remain standing, of course, even as the desert countryside of four continents bears the marks of the nuclear era. All appears well, at least on the surface. We can think about the future, because there is a future to think about. We can now shed our nihilism and go to church.

Or perhaps not. I think of the words of the late writer Susan Sontag, who spent her childhood in the Southwest and who conjured

> a permanent modern scenario: apocalypse looms, and it doesn't occur. . . . Apocalypse has become an event that is happening, and not happening. It may be that some of the most feared events, like those involving the irreparable ruin of the environment, have already happened. But we don't know it yet, because the standards have changed. Or because we do not have the right indexes for measuring the catastrophe. Or simply because this is a catastrophe in slow motion.

A catastrophe in slow motion: that sounds about right. The nuclear one has slowed down to a crawl, while the irreparable ruin of the environment continues apace. Rockets are aimed at us from Moscow and Almaty and perhaps Ürümqi, but they no longer seem real; Pax Coca-Cola reigns over the world; India and Pakistan and Iran are so far away. But for those of us who grew up in its frightening, long shadow, the Cold War will go on forever, like a desert highway. It endures. It is built into the landscape of the desert, and into our minds: Ground Zero, like the kingdom of heaven, will be forever within us.

From an aplomado's-eye view to a rocket's-eye view: the new landlord changed the way things worked down this way. When in 1954, at the height of the Cold War, the McGregor Range was extended north and west onto Otero Mesa to embrace an area of more than a thousand square miles, the land lost some of its people: about two hundred ranchers and smallholders were

20. A winter storm gathers over the Guadalupe Mountains east of Otero Mesa. Photograph by Gregory McNamee.

removed, a notable holdout being John Prather, a rancher who had worked the range for half a century and who refused the government's check to pack up and leave his place just south of the Sacramentos. He armed himself, and federal authorities wisely decided to work their way around him rather than risk the bad publicity of gunning him down. Prather stayed on Otero Mesa until his death in 1965; he is buried here. He figures in Edward Abbey's novel *Fire on the Mountain*, an inspiration for Thoreauvian (or, perhaps, armed Thoreauvian) resisters everywhere. He figures in spirit in Cormac McCarthy's more recent novel *Cities of the*

Plain, too, inhabiting a place of which one interlocutor says, "Mr Johnson says the army sent people out here with orders to survey seven states in the southwest and find the sorriest land they could find and report back. And Mac's ranch was settin right in the middle of it."

The army retains its domain on the mesa, other offices of the government much of the rest. As they have out in the Cabeza Prieta and the Mojave, our warriors have turned out to be good stewards of the land, coming out only now and again to drill and fire, otherwise leaving things alone. Said one soldier to Steve Strom and me on a visit in February 2007, "It's pretty quiet today, and Route 506 is open, sir. But please be advised that there will be maneuvers. So don't be alarmed if you see someone in Arab dress."

Otero Mesa is good country for many kinds of wildlife—desert bighorn sheep, antelope, deer, coyotes, lizards, and of course aplomados are on the roster—precisely because the military is so much a part of the place. It is just so closer to my home, in the Sonoran Desert country between Gila Bend and Yuma, Arizona, where the military blows the hell out of huge swaths of countryside designated a couple of decades ago as the Barry M. Goldwater Air Force Range. Periodically the air force carpet bombs it, the marines strafe it, and the army shells it, leaving a wake of detritus and destruction that only a scrap-metal dealer could love.

The military rarely announces this infernal visitation, and so it can catch an unwary visitor by surprise. This was the case for me back in the early winter of 1989, when, heading across the western desert somewhere near Mohawk, I happened on a sortie of bombers, helicopters, and fighters blasting a few miles of sand dunes into submission. Just a few weeks later, those same aircraft would be obliterating other sand dunes in a desert far away. I suppose their little firestorm off I-8 was useful practice for the dirty work ahead, preparation for a war for oil.

As with Otero Mesa, not many people live out this way. One who does, I hear, is an old college acquaintance of mine, famed in his day for prodigious experiments in altering reality. For obvious reasons, he must remain nameless, for his job, another friend from those times tells me, is now to observe and analyze the effects of the bombers' work from the safety of a bunker tucked into the desert hills. I have not been able to track him down, and I suspect that once you enter that kind of subterranean world, the last thing you would want to do is come up to the surface to answer some pesky writer's questions about the meaning of it all.

In any event, the result of all this destruction is

21. Silverleaf nightshade (*Solanum elaeagnifolium Cav.*) (detail). Photograph by Stephen Strom.

22. Otero Mesa grassland under an overcast sky. Photograph by Stephen Capra.

that the Gila Bend region is a haven for wildlife of all kinds. That may seem paradoxical, but it works this way, much as it does on the mesa: the bombing range is off-limits to tourists without official clearance, and that official clearance is hard to come by. No humans means no cars (a bighorn, I guess, can more easily hear an A-10 than the whine of a car engine), no shotguns, no dune buggies, no cross-country motorcycles, no beer-soaked off-roaders. Up against the mightiest military machine in the world, in other words, wildlife has a better chance of survival than it does against the average citizen, wrapped in the Second Amendment and armed to the teeth.

Thus is Otero Mesa in good shape, in at least some measure, because the Cold War kept it from other uses, kept its pronghorn and jackrabbits and cows off anyone's radar. For that we must be thankful, even if the situation is, well, laden with irony.

And so it is with the emergence of a new avatar of the military-industrial complex, one in which Arab dress figures prominently and wars once cold have become suddenly hot, again playing themselves out on the sandy grasslands of Otero Mesa. ▪

23. An oil pump at work on the New Mexico plains. Photograph by Stephen Capra.

Chapter 3

Oil

You smell it before you hear it: a smell of sulfur, and fire, smoke, and greasy water. It is infernal, pungent, unforgettable. The smell sinks into your nostrils, into your clothing, into your hair and skin. Days pass before the all-encompassing aroma disappears.

You hear it before you see it. There is the roar and hiss of excess gas being burned off—and, more quietly, the gasps of the animals who wander by when the pilot light goes off, as it will from time to time, and are asphyxiated. There is the crunching of the drill against rock, its whine alternating as it hits relatively harder and softer formations. There is the squealing of pipe sinking into the earth, the teeth-chattering grinding of gears, the hum of incessant engines. Writes the Texas novelist and historian Elmer Kelton, who grew up in an oil patch across the Pecos River, not so very far from here, "On crisp winter mornings we could hear the grinding and clanking of oilfield machinery from miles away, especially when pipe was being pulled from the hole and stacked inside a steel derrick." That was tranquil, compared to the horizon-filling noises modern drilling equipment can produce.

And then you see it: a forest of derricks stretching out across the sky, filling the creosote prairie, joined by roads cut across the dirt and grass. You see oil-stained pools of water everywhere, the unearthed remnants of ancient oceans. A good operator will return this water to the earth by way of a saltwater disposal well so carefully constructed that it will never find the level of fresh drinking water, but good operators are not always to be found, particularly in a time when good behavior is little rewarded economically or politically; and in all events, at least some portion of water manages to elude those who would channel it where it does not want to flow.

Again we have Kelton as a witness. He writes, "From an economic standpoint, cattle and oil are highly compatible, because a good oil well can pay for a considerable amount of feed. A standing joke says that the best mineral supplement for cattle is a working pump jack." Kelton adds, however, that, cattle being cattle, pools of oil from a broken pipeline or well spillage will draw a herd to drink just as surely as will a stock tank, meaning, in practice, the loss of more livestock than any pack of wolves could pull down. Oil companies large and small keep a fund to pay off cattle losses—and even the damage occasionally done to cowboys, tripped up by slush pits, discarded steel cable, rutted roads, and other artifacts of the industry, and to their horses, drowned in oil pits as surely as the victims of the La Brea pits.

And not just livestock. Not far from La Brea stands Beverly Hills High School—seen in dozens of films, including the canonical *It's a Wonderful Life*—where a disproportionate number of graduates have fallen ill with or died of various cancers over the years, well beyond the normal distribution of a cluster of diseases caused largely by environmental rather than genetic factors. For half a century, the school grounds had doubled as an oil field, with the city of Beverly Hills earning a sizable royalty for granting the privilege to a private energy developer. Workers at oil refineries and related facilities are notably susceptible to such illnesses, and now city-dwellers were to be poisoned by the on-site treatment of extracted oil with ammonia, radioactive iodine, and other toxic elements. New Mexico communities such as Lovington and Carlsbad have seen just the same thing, with groundwater contamination, a higher than statistically probable incidence of cancers of various kinds, and always, somewhere close by, spokespersons from industry and government insisting that it's nature's way and no one's to blame.

Poison, black water, lakes and spouts of fire, pestilence. As Texas playwright William Hauptman notes, oil country has "the feeling of a place where some great catastrophic event had taken place, like a battlefield."

24. Oil storage tanks. Photograph by Stephen Capra.

Such things inspire a hellish image—literally, for the Sumerian idea of hell that survives in our own vision of the underworld, that of a demonic place punctuated by fire and lightning, has a geological basis, born in a Mesopotamia that was tectonically quite active in the second millennium BC. Even now, the floodplain of the Tigris and Euphrates is laced with deposits of flammable gases that, helped along by subterranean volcanic and seismic activity, can send up jets of flame that flare like geysers on the desert, sights that would surely have suggested a frightening underworld to a storyteller of ages past. Some of these jets are still burning in places like Kirkuk, which Americans have recently become all too familiar with, thanks to decisions made by the Bush administration in the lofty realm of geopolitics—and petropolitics.

In January 2005, that administration, working through the Bureau of Land Management (BLM), authorized private firms to drill 225 oil and gas wells on Otero Mesa. The move was no surprise; immediately after the election of 2004, in which the president trumpeted that he had earned political capital and was going to spend it, loyalist legislators and White House staffers hastened to push through a program of resource development that repudiated existing regulations such as the Endangered Species Act and the Clean Air Act. The president himself made it clear that his administration would oppose any effort to fight regulations governing carbon monoxide emissions and the like, while his appointees in the Environmental Protection Agency sought to undo the listing process for species threatened by development by, in effect, making it impossible for scientists to prove that a species was in fact in danger. In a truncated process of consideration, the public comment that came to the BLM was more than 85 percent opposed to drilling on Otero Mesa, those numbers reflecting a once unlikely alliance of ranchers, hunters, environmentalists, and property rights advocates. The numbers did not move the administration, which had long since proved itself to be contemptuous of the very idea of popular will or of the democratic majority.

In a matter of some irony—irony being the hallmark of the administration, at least to outside observers—the BLM, after the first test well was drilled there in 1997,

concluded that Otero Mesa had "a low potential for economically recoverable amounts of oil and gas." That has not kept the agency, responding to political pressure, from opening most of the mesa to development, even if three of the five natural gas wells that were subsequently drilled turned out to be nonproductive. But that is the nature of the enterprise: more than half of the land leased from the government for oil and gas development in the West—at last count, about thirty-five million acres—is not being used: only fifty thousand wells are now sited on those public lands, far below capacity. Put another way, the industry already has too many leases to know what to do with: of the thirty-six million acres leased nationwide, only twelve million are under production. By any calculus this means, among other things, that there is no need whatever to open up still other lands. The situation is as if the government had built ten identical shopping malls side by side, then, worrying that the individual malls were too little frequented by shoppers, decided that the solution would be to build ten more, since the free market dictates that there should be plenty of shopping malls to serve the interest of the owning class.

The oil and gas industry, glad for the accommodation, increasingly pressures the government to open up the public domain to private interests. The present government obliges, for one of its sworn tenets is that government itself is evil and needs to be replaced by a putatively benevolent private sector: from free markets, the ideologues argue, comes freedom, never mind that these markets are rigged to begin with. The short-term result of this embarrassment of potential riches may be one that will come back to bite the investors: too little of the land is productive for their purposes, and the only sure way to find that out is to sink test wells—and large quantities of money in the bargain.

But the result will surely come back to bite the land. Drilling causes damage of many kinds: every wellhead requires the clearing of three to five acres of land, so that, to implement the administration's initial program, some 1,125 acres of Otero Mesa would likely have to be bladed clean. To connect these wellheads to one another and to the outside world, roads must be built, good solid asphalt roads that can bear heavy truck traffic in all weathers. Build roads, particularly in places where wildlife travel—herds of pronghorn moving from pasture to pasture, flocks of migratory birds passing overhead—and you create fragmented habitat, a vexing problem for anyone seeking to remediate damaged country years later. Fragmentation has an inexorable logic: with it comes a slow lessening of the numbers and kinds of animals and plants in an area, a lessening that quickens in crisis and that almost always ends in extinction. If you want to kill a place, in other words, subdivide it and put a road down and you're almost there.

In the meanwhile, the rush is on. Florida's senior senator recently agreed to support drilling in the West, including the ravaged North Slope of Alaska, so long as the Bush administration agreed in turn not to drill off Florida's coast for the next seven years. Virginia, conversely, has approved drilling in its waters, as if the Old Dominion had a place in OPEC. Tom DeLay, House majority leader until his ouster in 2006, allowed that the rush to drill elsewhere, in places such as Otero Mesa, was in part a symbolic exercise meant to show that the administration and then ruling party could do pretty much whatever they wished.

But on Otero Mesa, the rush is anything but symbolic. New Mexico's oldest petroleum producer, a major donor to the Republican Party at all levels, has been a force in pushing for the land to be opened for development. The company, a force as well in state politics—no surprise, since New Mexico ranks second in natural gas production and fifth in oil production among the states—has long been accustomed to getting its way, and in all events, as a New Mexico senatorial aide told environmentalist Steve Capra, "We see you guys three or four times a year, but we see the oil companies every week."

Oil has been the prime currency of political mastery for less than a century, since 1911, when Winston Churchill made the fateful decision to convert the Royal Navy from burning Welsh coal to burning oil from the Persian Gulf. Oil was central to the conduct of World War I, when tanks and warplanes made their wide-scale debut on the battlefield. It helped precipitate World War II, as the United States—then one of the world's leading exporters—cut off supplies of oil to Japan and as Hitler's forces sought a quick hold on the great oil fields of the Caucasus. Oil has determined the fate of nations: consider the fortunes of Aramco, a company led by a consortium of American investors that managed through considerable guile to insert itself in territory tightly controlled by the British—thanks, in part, to the labors of one H. St. John Philby, a British spy and double agent who held great influence in the court of Saudi king Ibn Saud, and who would become a more faithful servant of Standard Oil than of his government. The Americans won Saudi favor not only through

Philby, but also through an intrepid Chicago-born entrepreneur and diplomat named Charles Crane, who did for Ibn Saud what the British failed to do: Crane built a costly waterworks that brought drinking water into the Saudi interior. (For his part, Philby obtained the monopoly on selling Ford automobiles in the country. In six years he sold the king 1,450 cars.) The result was a concession to the American concern for what the U.S. State Department once called "the most valuable commercial prize in the history of the planet," namely, the vast oil fields of Arabia; for an initial investment of one hundred thousand pounds, Aramco eventually extracted more than a trillion dollars from the Arabian reserves while forging a state that remains of key strategic importance today.

Just so, the shah of Iran came into power after the CIA engineered a coup meant to keep Persian oil in capitalism's hands, just as the president of Egypt gained regional influence by standing up to Britain and France and seized the Suez Canal in order to protect the oil route from Persia to Europe. A generation later, with American aid, an ambitious soldier named Saddam Hussein seized and consolidated power. Not long afterward, Hussein having tried in the meanwhile to reclaim the lost province of Kuwait for his country, American forces were arrayed in battle against him. They returned a dozen years later, and acre-feet of blood were shed.

Writing in his book *Blood and Oil: The Dangers and Consequences of America's Growing Petroleum Dependency* (2004), national-security scholar Michael T. Klare observes that the real wars of today are not about clashes of civilizations and ideologies, but about natural resources. "In Angola and Sierra Leone," Klare writes, "it was control of the diamond fields that sustained the bloodshed for so long; in the Congo, gold and copper; in Borneo and Cambodia, timber." Now, in many parts of the world, the battle is over oil, a conflict that is reshaping American policy across the spectrum, such that "the U.S. military is being converted into a global oil-protection service." Much diplomatic effort, to say

25. Oil storage tanks and seepage. Photograph by Stephen Capra.

Chapter 3

nothing of the work of the military, is now invested in "securitizing" oil and wooing its producers into the American camp, even as America loses more and more of its credibility in the world at large thanks to a politics best described by a bumper sticker I once saw, incongruously, in archconservative Catron County, New Mexico: "Yee-haw is not a foreign policy," it read. The contours of that great battle over oil are only now taking shape; what is certain is that America is becoming ever more dependent on foreign sources of oil, and thus increasingly vulnerable, as Klare writes, "to the violence and disorder that accompanies oil production in politically unstable and often hostile producers."

Slightly more than half of the domestic oil demand in 2000 was met with foreign product; by 2025, that figure is expected to rise to 67.9 percent, or nearly twenty million barrels per day. Satisfying these needs will introduce conflict into regions whose rulers may tolerate us but whose people do not; this is true of the Persian Gulf, and it may also be true of the so-called

Alternative Eight, nations such as Mexico, Colombia, and Nigeria, whose political futures are anything but certain, even if they were to meet the happy predictions of American policy analysts and policy makers and produce enough to sustain our desperately wanton habits of energy consumption. More likely they will not, of course, and more likely the petroleum-producing nations will instead become ever more hostile to American demands for more and more oil.

The search for new sources of energy has thus become ever more urgent, and it is taking place in what has hitherto been terra incognita. Africa, for instance, has long gone ignored almost everywhere outside Africa, but now that oil is scarcer and the continent has plenty of it, drillers and diplomats are paying attention. Since 1990, John Ghazvinian observes in his recent book *Untapped: The Scramble for Africa's Oil* (2007), the petroleum industry—read large, to include wildcat drillers and independents as well as Big Oil—has invested twenty billion dollars in exploration and development in Africa. In the years from 2007 to 2010, another fifty billion will be spent, mostly to expand the production capabilities in the Gulf of Guinea, a nearly ideal location, offshore and thus perhaps not subject to the whims of landlubber dictators and corrupt officialdom and civil wars, things that plague places such as Sierra Leone and Nigeria, while also astride easily accessible sea lanes leading to Europe and the Americas. Yet, because of the rich reserves of sweet oil that the Gulf of Guinea holds, certainly as compared to the relatively sour oil of places such as the North Sea and the Permian Basin, West Africa is now being overrun and contested; Nigeria and Angola jockey for political dominance in places such as São Tomé and Príncipe, shady neocolonialists wander the streets of West Africa's capitals, and everywhere one looks China is suddenly a major presence, having smartly committed to foreign aid and infrastructure development while the West was looking the other way. Given all the tumult, it is no surprise that the Gulf of Guinea has

become, as Osama bin Laden once predicted, a fertile recruiting ground for al-Qaeda and other Islamist organizations dedicated to the creation of oil-rich states with medieval governments.

Then there is Central Asia. A power that wishes for what the military calls "full-spectrum dominance" of the world cannot overlook the vast region that runs from Turkey to China, a region writhing with fundamentalists and clanging with Kalashnikovs. In that scenario, the American invasion of Iraq can be seen as less about countering terrorism than paving the way for dominance over resources, principally oil. There is a developing "New Great Game," the old one being the race between Russia and Great Britain for control of Central Asia, that is now playing out between East and West, and more pointedly between the three poles of fundamentalist Islam, a protective Russia, and an energy-hungry United States. China figures in there, too, as does Iran, a serious contender in the geopolitical scheme of things. The Caspian Sea basin is perhaps

26. Pronghorn (*Antilocapra americana*) grazing on Otero Mesa. Photograph by Gregory McNamee.

the world's biggest untapped source of fossil fuel reserves, at least three times larger than stores within the United States; this surely explains why American interests began working in the 1990s to build a pipeline from the bizarre dictatorship of Turkmenistan through Taliban-controlled Afghanistan and on to the Indian Ocean, much to the annoyance of the Russian government.

When confronted with such realities, governments have tended to guard the interests of the multinationals within their borders. In scenarios such as these, war seems the logical outcome; the question now is mostly one of who will be pulling the triggers. All this need not be, but to avert conflict requires that America develop alternative sources of energy and a comprehensive blueprint for the postpetroleum era, for a time when petroleum and other fossil fuels are finally recognized as being at a dangerous premium. Instead, just at the moment, we have a politics in which oil and oilmen reign supreme, and when they offer a plan at all, it is for more of the same: more consumption, more dependency, more conflict, more blood over oil.

Against this big-picture backdrop, Otero Mesa is an admittedly distant and minor battlefield. Yet it is part of that big picture all the same, and it is of critical importance in its own right. Less well publicized than the threatened wildlife preserves on the North Slope of Alaska, it has been slated for sacrifice only because it offers a tiny stopgap in a Hobbesian time of scarcity—or, perhaps better, a time when a Hobbesian vision of the future is being pushed upon us, demanding that we gather still more resources for our use before someone else gets to them, a greedy, desperate scramble in the war of each against all.

Oil is always an attraction in ranching country, as Elmer Kelton recounts; it can pay for a lot of cattle fodder indeed, buy a new truck, pay off a mortgage. To see a ranch that does not have a pump working off in some corner or another is unusual in parts of the country where oil is present, largely because many ranches are a patchwork of public and private land on which multiple leases have been signed, in keeping with the doctrine of multiple use that drives most federal agencies with any jurisdiction over the public domain. Take a look at some of the little places out on Otero Mesa, particularly in the southern reaches projected to host oil wells, and it is easy to see how oil might be attractive: ranching, after all, is about the hardest way there is to make an honest living, as anyone who has ever set foot on a ranch quickly learns. A story from West Texas, from about 1920, tells the tale: A traveler spends the night on a dryland ranch and, surveying the dust and dead trees come sunlight, asks the rancher, "How in the world do you make a go of things at all?" The rancher, pointing to the hired man who is sitting down to his breakfast of grits and boiled coffee, says, "You see that fella there? Well, he works for me and I can't pay him. In two years he gets the ranch. Then I work for him till I get it back."

Linn and Tweeti Blancett, ranchers in the San Juan Basin of northwestern New Mexico, live on just such a patchwork, and they have witnessed at close hand the effects of oil on the land. "We are overrun by more

27. An oil storage tank with a leakage pond. Photograph by Stephen Capra.

than five hundred active gas wells," they recount.

Each well pad and access road gobbles up about three acres of grazing land. Gas gathering and distribution pipelines transect our property everywhere. Pipelines are not reseeded, roads are built too wide without adequate drainage, and surface spills are not cleaned up. Cheat grass and thistle sprouts all over the pipeline scars, making the ground unusable for grazing. . . . At the well pads, the waste pits and compressors are unfenced or so poorly fenced that cattle and wildlife can drink from the pits and drip pans. Uncovered drip pans hold ethylene glycol and water, a sweet-tasting beverage that kills livestock and wildlife that drink from it. We lose several cows a year due to these hazards. Since well operators are reluctant to pay for livestock losses and require proof that the animal was killed as a result of their operations, we must have each animal autopsied and examined for hydrocarbon residues and cause of death. That doesn't even count all the fees for lawyers and other experts we pay to collect damages from the oil companies.

Their neighbor Jake Hottle adds,

I remember as a child having clean water in our well. In the '50s, oil and gas began drilling up and down the Animas River corridor. After graduating in 1965, I spent three years in the military in electronics. I will always remember while here on visits, my mother standing at the sink trying to drink the stinking water coming from our well in the late 1960s. She passed away in 1974 at sixty-four years old. I believe poorly cemented gas wells played a role in her early death. Upon returning home in 1979, my

wife and I began to notice there was a tremendous amount of cancer in the families who lived in my neighborhood. Upon investigation, we found poorly cemented wells, open pit dumping, and methane gas in 40 percent of the water wells tested.

Near Carlsbad, not far from the national park, Roy and Louise Dearing, respectively a retired oil and gas worker and homemaker, bought a country place in the 1980s. "There was always a small compressor there, about five hundred feet from the house," they recall, "but when Duke Energy bought the land a few years ago, they replaced that little 100 horsepower compressor with one that has 1200 horsepower. If it doesn't break down it runs twenty-four hours a day, every day. . . . It's like living next door to an airport."

The Dearings, like the Blancetts and Jake Hottle, are anything but the city-slicker environmentalists whom well-funded antienvironmental groups such as

People for the West once conjured as bogeymen, urban enemies who would arrive with their lawsuits and keep ordinary people from making a living so that little owls could flourish. Even so, the energy companies have singled out these country people, natives of the places in which they work, as outside agitators and radicals, disgruntled NIMBYs with a sense of privilege. This, happily, has had the effect of making them even more active in their opposition. The Dearings, for instance, took their arguments to New Mexico's congressional delegation in Washington, called press conferences, made videotapes, and took photographs. In the end they sued and won, putting their life savings at risk in order to press their right to live on that freest of free markets, their own land.

They are unusual, of course, in their willingness to take such risks. And the good guys do not always win. "Can we make a difference?" asks Carlsbad high school counselor Israel Palma. "I don't know. It seems like they always win. It's hard to fight the big money boys."

It is, and the big money boys count on that, just as the government counts on people's taking the path of least resistance and refusing to speak out about the issues that concern them.

Against those who have suffered from the oil industry, the Bureau of Land Management happily claims that it insists on environmentally sensitive resource development. The oil companies make the same claims. Yet anyone with eyes can see that, apart from a few showcase venues, development means damage and all too often no effort to undo the harm— whence ravaged mountains and dead seas, pools of standing oil and chemicals and boneyards full of dead cattle. As I write, one seven-million-acre oil-producing district in New Mexico is assigned one, precisely one, BLM inspector, who cannot possibly hope to cover that ground. This is no surprise in a climate where industry is entrusted with the business of regulating itself, a fox-guarding-the-henhouse privilege that not even the robber barons of the Gilded Age dared hope for, but it casts in grave doubt the sincerity of any claims that development is being done with a careful eye out for the health of the land.

Let us imagine what will happen if the Hobbesian vision of distant capital succeeds. The air over Otero Mesa will reek and rumble. Its quiet dirt roads will become paved highways, laden with trucks and lined with roadkill. Its yellow-throated blackbirds and aplomado falcons will go elsewhere, silenced by the thunder of compressors and the whine of engines. Its cattle will die, and the chances are good that the people who tend to those cattle will, too. A new pipeline will snake its way across the mesa, taking oil and gas off to energy-thirsty California. Somewhere, one or two people will celebrate the profits—or political capital—they have earned, but in the end they will die, too, and probably without ever having set eyes on the place that has died to serve them.

The world is running on empty, warns the noted petroleum geologist Kenneth Deffeyes, and yet Humvees continue to roll down the assembly lines, roads to be built, and economic models in which oil figures at the center to be churned out. That scarcity has a name: Hubbert's peak, a term that refers not to an oil-implicated place along the lines of Kuwait or Teapot Dome, but to a statistical concept hatched in the 1950s by another geologist, M. King Hubbert. It posits that world oil production over time will follow the classic bell curve, the apex of which took place somewhere in the past century of production. Tinkering with Hubbert's math just a little, Deffeyes, writing in late 2004, projected that the end of 2005 would see total oil production at 2.013 trillion barrels, which was just about right. He then added, provocatively, that Thanksgiving of that year ought to be designated World Oil Peak Day and that First Worlders use the occasion to give thanks for the years 1901 to 2004, when oil was abundant and comparatively cheap, despite a few hiccups in the world system—World War II, the OPEC embargo, and the like. Stopgap measures will not help, he offered: drilling the five billion barrels locked up in the Arctic National Wildlife Refuge, as the Bush administration has been clamoring to do for years, will only put off the nation's thirst for a few months at best.

Otero Mesa's reserves are far fewer. Trapped underneath its porous limestone and deep sands, there is fuel enough only to last, at best, half a month—about a trillion cubic feet. That figure may be wildly generous, for other estimates put the mesa's store of gas at only 110 billion cubic feet. Either is a proverbial drop in a bucket, considering how many buckets it takes to slake humankind's thirst.

Even so, powerful interests are arrayed against Otero Mesa and the rest of the earth, aided and abetted by an administration founded on oil and a millenarian vision that promises heaven for those who destroy the ground beneath them. Let us call these people what they are. They are devourers who talk benignly of consumption as they use up much, much more than their share. They are gluttons, if gluttons who work out daily at the gym to disguise the evidence of their appetites. They are men and women who deny themselves absolutely nothing, no matter what the expense, an expense that is always borne by other people and by the earth itself. They are killers of places and landscapes and the people and animals and plants that inhabit them, whose existence is a nuisance. They talk patriotism while destroying the ground on which America was built. They are thieves who would rob the future, for which they have no regard in any event, in order to nurse the past.

That past has been extraordinarily profitable for them; it has built empires, financial and political, for them and their kind, and, naturally enough, they have a hard time letting it go. Moreover, they believe that by divine ordination you and I should make possible the eternal continuation of the good times. Their efforts to prop up an unsustainable

28. A working oil field to the east of Otero Mesa. Photograph by Stephen Capra.

economy and an insupportable way of life that even friendly industry analysts agree is rapidly passing would be touching were it not so damaging: not for nothing has it been observed that even if the earth can support five billion human beings, it has trouble satisfying the endless appetites of three hundred million Americans, who use twenty million barrels of oil per day, a quarter of the world's production, mostly in the form of gasoline, mostly to move them and their things around.

They are the enemy. Or, I should say, we are the enemy, since, moving ourselves and our things around with them, we are all implicated in this system of waste and destruction.

Is there another way? Of course. The future is unwritten. In the very short term, governments can make it an urgent, war-footing matter to find soft-path, renewable, clean, safe sources of energy and encourage forms of settlement, commerce, and transportation that allow people to stay close to their work and food to be grown close to its consumers. Ordinary consumers can learn to turn off lights, eat foods that don't require tons of pesticides and shipping far distances out of season, and stop buying gas-guzzling vehicles.

We have a very long way to go before the nation can become energy independent, a long way to go before we even reach less than profligate status. Yet the energy industry has historically shown itself to be capable of turning on a dime, and even if the leading producers have recently resisted regulations requiring greater efficiencies, the need for a new energy regime has to be evident to even the most casual observer. That transformation may well be perilous, politically and economically; previous transformations have been profoundly dislocating, but the nation has weathered through them. Yet more dislocating will be the worldwide economic shock when the news sinks in that depletion and scarcity are the order of the day, when it finally becomes clear that Hubbert's peak has been passed. The change will be painful, almost certainly. But change is also necessary, and Otero Mesa, that windswept, faraway grassland, speaks for many of the reasons why that should be true.

Three decades ago, Jimmy Carter installed a solar water heater on the White House roof, donned a cardigan, and announced that the ongoing energy crisis was "the moral equivalent of war." One of Ronald Reagan's first acts as president was to order the heater removed, and during his tenure Department of Energy support for research into solar buildings fell from one hundred million dollars to just one million. Matters have not improved in the years since, and subsequent administrations of whatever political stripe have been no better at exploring alternative sources of energy. As I write, on Independence Day of the year 2007, the House of Representatives is deliberating on legislation to implement tough efficiency standards for lighting and appliances, expand biofuels research, and fund carbon capture and storage; yet all the proposals on the table fail to mention fuel-economy standards, anathema to politicians in the auto-manufacturing and energy-producing states. So it is that there are more than 250 million vehicles on America's roads today to serve a population of three hundred million people and perhaps another 400 million vehicles traversing roads elsewhere in the world.

Those vehicles are thirsty. They scream for fossil fuel. We all scream for fossil fuel. If we do not change our course, then Otero Mesa will die—just as every other place is dying, measurably, daily, inarguably, before our very eyes.

If not now, when? ◼

29. Pepperweed (*Lepidium latifolium L.*) and fleabane (*Erigeron philadelphicus*). Photograph by Stephen Strom.

30. Wildflower mix in springtime. Photograph by Stephen Strom.

Chapter 4

Otero Mesa and the Fate of the Land

Thirty years ago, on a train crossing the coastal plain of southern Italy, I fell into conversation with a man about my age who had earned a fortune by buying old dockside warehouses in London and selling them as luxury apartments to people who had been busily earning fortunes of their own. He asked where I was from. When I told him I hailed from the Southwest, he smiled and said, "I've been there, once. Quite a beautiful place, really. All that extraordinary, beautiful land, but"—here he paused meaningfully—"there's nothing on it."

"Well," I replied, gazing out at the snarled macchia and tangled drifts of prickly Apulian cactus, "you're off by a word: all that extraordinary, beautiful land, *and* there's nothing on it."

We continued to exchange pleasantries, watching out the window as the cactus-studded landscape— apart from the occasional castles and piazzas quite reminiscent of the desert borderlands of southern Arizona and New Mexico—rolled by. And as it did, I thought of the borderland places I have known, some, though scarred by the human quest for wealth, still harboring pronghorn and cougars, ringtails and bighorn sheep, places that, as Ernest Hemingway insisted, are worth fighting for.

That bar-car conversation took place in less chewed-up times, long before my desert city had mushroomed from a quarter-million to a million people, a metastasis my old friend Edward Abbey correctly foresaw three decades ago. Ed is buried out in the Cabeza Prieta, another wild and lonely place, and I imagine that he is busily turning over in his grave even as thousands of footsteps erode it away.

Tucson still felt like a Southwestern city back then. Alamogordo was tiny. Las Cruces was still a small town

31. The Shiloh Hills, in east-central Otero Mesa. Photograph by Stephen Strom.

separated by miles and minutes of empty space from El Paso. But then, forty-odd years ago, when the world was young, I lived on the very edge of the desert in El Paso; beyond my family's little house on Cielo Vista Drive there wasn't much but rock, sand, and claret cup cacti and, far off beyond the horizon, the shimmering promise of Van Horn. Cielo Vista Drive is surrounded by city now, and El Paso stretches out to that horizon; from Otero Mesa, on a clear night, you can see its lights shimmering, a lure for Cormac McCarthy's cowboys. Smog blankets the desert all the way to the Glass Mountains and McKittrick Canyon. Sewage trucked in from New York City dries on the flanks of the Sierra Blanca. There is talk of adding radioactive waste to the mix. The salamanders of Barton Springs, the jewel of faraway Austin, are in danger of extinction, while the Cornudas Mountains land snail shows no signs of expanding its territory to embrace neighboring rises. The Rio Grande has slowed to a trickle from Colorado to the Gulf of Mexico. Albuquerque is swelling like a tick, and Phoenix is bloated beyond recognition. About the only thing there's no shortage of in the Southwest, and everywhere else for that matter, is realtors and developers whose business it is to fill up all the empty

32. The Shiloh Hills near Cornucopia Draw. Photograph by Stephen Strom.

spaces so as to fill up a bank account to take off to some un-filled-up spot—La Jolla is always a favorite—and get away from the crowds they've helped create.

Solitude, the possibility of quiet, of escape, is being lost daily and is well on the way to disappearing entirely. Hemmed in, we have begun to lose territory to overrun, too. We have used a lot of space, we humans, have used up more than our share of resources; indeed, in a little more than a century, we have used the human species' share of resources of certain kinds, not least of them fossil fuels. Now is the time to learn to do more with less. Time to leave what is left of the world alone.

Those with a voice, it has been said, have a moral duty to speak for the voiceless. I have long taken as my beat the possibilities of resurrection, of bringing again to life what we have destroyed through our history—the Library of Alexandria, the Aral Sea, thousands of lost species, thousands of lost languages, thousand of lost peoples, thousands of lost rivers. If we are ever to come close to bringing back the better past for a better future, then we must have at least some country about which cartographers can write, as their medieval peers did, only the words, "Beyond here lie dragons." I want places in which the historian who called American history one continuous real-estate transaction would for once be proven wrong, places where, if it comes to it, in the battle between cows and condominiums—or between dogies and derricks—the cows win every time out.

There are times when such hopes seem impossibly naive. Consider a recent report from the Nature Conservancy, which estimates that as of 1995—a full dozen years ago—only 17 percent of the world's land area remained truly wild, absent of humans, crops, roads, lights. The report continues that half of the world's surface area is used for crops or grazing, that more than half of all forests have been lost to land converted to agricultural use or urbanized. In the meanwhile, the largest land mammals on almost every continent have been eliminated, while, owing to damming, nearly six times as much water is held in artificial storage worldwide as flows freely. We live in a time of disappearance, destruction, extinction. We live, as Aldo Leopold warned more than half a century ago, in a world of wounds.

There are a few wild places left. Some of them I have seen: Kamchatka and the Gobi from the air, many others from the ground. I am happy not to visit them again, to let them go about their ancient business without me, with the thought that one less human might be one more day of survival. In one, the Gila Wilderness of southwestern New Mexico, I once spent a full-moon vigil across a glade from a female mountain lion who studied me with casual indifference, yawning repeatedly to air her lack of concern that I had invaded her place. (It is possible, of course, that she was testing the air for scent and concluded that I would be just too gamey a snack.) In another, the Swansea Wilderness of western Arizona, on a fine, warm late March evening, my only company was a curious kit fox who scampered into my campsite to examine the unaccustomed light of my campfire. He did not know enough to mistrust humans, and I still feel pangs of shame for having disturbed his solitude. On Otero Mesa, I have been amazed to spend time in the presence of pronghorn

33. Grass, with the Cornudas Mountains in the background. Photograph by Stephen Capra.

that, like the kit fox, seem to have seen few enough cars and trucks that one such lumbering beast crossing their horizon did not constitute a threat—even though, of course, it did, if only indirectly.

I want to know that many more such places exist, that we still live in a world that can imaginatively accommodate the wild, the unasphalted, the unexploited, places that, to the shame of the capitalist system, have not been put to work making money for someone to cart off someplace else. Thus my new demand of developers, were I ever to gain a position of power to put it into place: you may develop away, build and extract whatever you like, but ninety-nine cents of every dollar you make has to stay in the place where it's made. Thus schools for Alamogordo and Dell City, not luxury villas in La Jolla and Tuscany. Thus the makings of a fine local economy, not the abandoned desert colonies of the past, the company towns of companies long moved on.

You cannot eat scenery. You cannot feast on the unharnessed wind or slurp up water hidden away far below the earth. But neither can you eat if all the food has moved elsewhere. In the end, if all the oil is pulled from Otero Mesa, it will serve to feed only a handful of hungry ghosts—and as for hungry machines, it will satisfy them for only a few days, which makes the notion of sacrificing this place to that end all the more irrational, as all vices are.

Otero Mesa is not pristine, not by any means. It is not wilderness, has not been so for many generations. It is not terra incognita, even if you have to find a fine-scaled map to get a sense of it from anywhere but the mesa itself. Many species have gone from it over the long course of time. Its agaves go ungathered, the people who once did that taxing work having found other ways of life. The army bombs it now and again. But for all that it is a fine place, a necessary place, deserving of much better than sacrifice for the profit of a privileged and well-connected few

34. Yucca (*Yucca treculeana*) flower. Photograph by Stephen Strom.

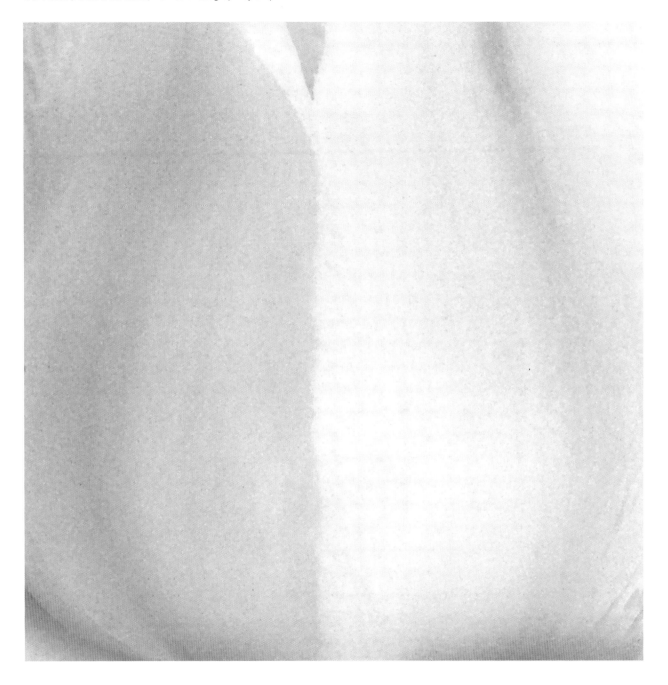

whose names most of us will never know.

Properly viewed, Otero Mesa would be conceived of and valued as a national treasure, one of the nation's most threatened ecosystems. Properly viewed, all the public domain would be seen in the same light and jealously protected from private exploitation.

Yet the mesa endures, even if largely unhonored. It continues to ward off the desert that has swallowed so much grassland. It continues to do all the real work it is meant to do, which is to be as it is, a remote plain of grass, the last of its kind until we can turn to the possibilities of resurrecting other places of its kind throughout the Chihuahuan Desert.

That day, I trust, will come, for in places like Otero Mesa lies the geography of hope: the preservation of vast, unquantifiable, unknowable sweeps of extraordinary, beautiful land—*and* with nothing on it.

Lance Armstrong, the great bicycle racer, burns as much energy as a handheld hair dryer. So does a cheetah running at full clip. Our brains use about as much as a refrigerator bulb, whether we're thinking hard or barely sentient. Those twinned facts should not keep us from devoting much thought to how we humans are going to unpaint ourselves from the corner we're in vis-à-vis fossil fuels: all of us owe it to the future to think—and hard—about what we can do on a micro- and macroscale to lessen our footprints on the land. We know all about the laws of thermodynamics and the geology of petroleum, coal, and other energy resources; we know that the thermodynamically more efficient survive in the Darwinian arena that is the world. The world's people use nearly eighty million barrels of oil a day, a poster case of thermodynamic inefficiency, and there is much work to do if we are to counteract the baleful effects of our addiction to irreplaceable fossil fuels and thereby regain the future. The most important alternative is brainpower, helped along by the wind, the sun, the sea, and other "soft," endlessly renewable sources of energy.

35. Looking south toward Alamo, Wind, and Flat Top mountains. Photograph by Stephen Capra.

36. Pepperweed (*Lepidium latifolium L.*) in springtime. Photograph by Stephen Strom.

And in the meanwhile, what is to be done about this place called Otero Mesa, this American Serengeti, this rare and threatened grassland?

The first best thing to do is to leave Otero Mesa alone, leave its handful of ranching families and visitors to keep an eye on a place that, if all goes well, will remain forever little visited. That is just as it should be, and even in this teeming, swarming, overpopulated nation, that is how it must be.

There are other possibilities, of course, that may unfold over the years to come. One is to use Otero Mesa as a laboratory for a better future. The low passes down by Dell City, for instance, where oil wells now twinkle in some mind's eye, are ideally situated to host windmills for generating electrical power. There, as with so much of the mesa country, the wind never stops blowing; as a storekeeper said to me on a typically blustery afternoon, "Days like this, there just isn't enough hairspray." It may be one of the smaller ironies of life that West Texas—the home of our oil industry and power base for a presidential administration with close ties to it—is among the nation's leading producers of wind-generated electricity, but it is, and that same wind comes whipping along into southern New Mexico, so hard, locals say, that if it ever stopped all the cows would fall over. Even as the oil economists talk gloomily of resource shortages and the effects of Hubbert's peak, the wind blows endlessly, with no end in sight.

Strong winds are common in every desert of the world, for it is the uneven distribution of solar energy that drives them—and solar energy, of course, is in no shortage in the dry country. The winds blow steadily in the comparatively mild season; come spring, when the earth begins to warm toward summer and its stormy season, they blow ever harder. The native people here tell of water serpents that dwell in the boiling summer clouds, bringing rain to the dry earth not in nourishing drops but in great black undulating curtains of water, leaving floods and destruction in their wake, led in, because the storms are blind, by helpful seeing winds. Witness a monsoon rain on Otero Mesa, and you will know just what that means. Those winds, those great storms, in every desert on earth, resist the tendency of all things to slip away into inertia and entropy; instead, they swell, burst, spawn new winds and new storms. They are frightening, powerful, destructive—and they provide a solution.

What is on or above Otero Mesa, of course, is not what has attracted so much attention, but what is under it. Here, again, we have choices. Underneath portions of the mesa may be a couple of weeks' worth of petroleum. The mesa as a whole, however, that great reef of filtering and purifying limestone, overlies what hydrologists now say is New Mexico's largest fresh-water aquifer, almost certainly more than eighteen trillion gallons of water, enough to sustain whole cities for hundreds of years into the future. That is the consequence of all those millions of years of water that have spilled, drop by drop and flake by flake, off the Sacramentos, the Guadalupes, the Shiloh Hills, down onto the mesa.

People, it almost—almost—goes without saying, cannot drink oil, whereas water is one of the few true necessities of life, and in a Southwest whose available water resources are nearly exhausted, the existence of so much water will be of tremendous importance to the region's future.

Determining how to use that water and for what purposes will almost certainly develop into another battle, if history is any guide, but the point remains: water trumps oil, and to develop that oil would be to jeopardize that water, cause enough for a necktie party in days past—if history is indeed any guide. What is more certain is that if oil and gas development is allowed on Otero Mesa, drilling will eventually break a seal in the limestone-lined aquifers far below the surface, polluting the groundwater and making it unusable for millions of years to come.

Limestone transports water, but also pollutants,

37. A rainbow forms in a summer monsoon storm over Otero Mesa. Photograph by Stephen Capra.

38. Hillsides with ocotillo (*Fouquieria splendens*) near Cornucopia Draw. Photograph by Stephen Strom.

very effectively, and the smallest error can easily create a natural catastrophe. The history of petroleum exploration and exploitation abounds with examples of destructive errors and their consequences, from which the overarching lesson to draw is this: to entrust so great a treasure as Otero Mesa's water to the oil industry is to invite disaster, period.

Water trumps oil in any sane reckoning of the world's resources. Yet when Otero County's commissioners began to enact regulations to protect that groundwater, BLM head and political appointee Kathleen Clarke wrote a sharply worded note informing them that the agency would ignore any ordinances that local governments cared to put into law if they impeded the quest for oil and gas. That is evidence enough, if more were needed, that the priorities of the ruling administration, staffed by ideologues, do not square with the governed—or of the public domain under its trust.

Another possibility is this: Otero Mesa, as part of

a larger complex of plains and mountains, makes an attractive venue for the reintroduction of many now extinct or extirpated animals, from often discussed ones such as the jaguar and wolf to the decidedly more offbeat menagerie proposed by advocates of "Pleistocene rewilding"—that is, bringing back creatures such as the camel and mammoth, possibly adding to the mix cheetahs, elephants, Przewalski's horse, and other exotic creatures that are endangered elsewhere. The notion may seem a little far-fetched—but then, so was introducing the oryx to this place. This is one of those houses of the mind that has to be built brick by brick, but the point is that in this still largely unfragmented landscape lie the necessary preconditions for such big-picture dreams, affording ample room for brainpower and imagination in discussions of its future.

In 2005 biologists reintroduced the Bolson tortoise to a private ranch not far from Otero Mesa. Those great reptiles, some weighing a hundred pounds and more, had disappeared from the mesa and elsewhere in the

Chihuahuan Desert ten thousand years ago, victims of both hunters and climate change; they have since been confined to a small portion of central Mexico. The Bolson tortoise is but a little part of a big puzzle; make room for the late Pleistocene camel and the Mexican gray wolf, make room for the desert bighorn sheep and the black-footed ferret, make room for a flotilla of aplomados, and Otero Mesa and its larger region become that much more whole, offering proof that we can undo at least some of the damage we have done to this generous and forgiving planet.

These are things for the people of Otero Mesa, and the people who have made Otero Mesa part of their landscapes, to decide in the fullness of time. The ranchers here, in the main, have been good caretakers of the land, precisely because they have to be; all you need do is spend time on the mesa, and you'll see plenty of evidence of their attentiveness to the land. The ranchers themselves are a part of this ecosystem; they are right for this place, and they belong here, working and tending to the land. Their domains, while seemingly vast to a hemmed-in and land-poor urbanite, are appropriate in scale, worked by people and not machines. The men and women and children who live here have made the land their own, know every stone and yucca, stalk and turn of the road; they are not corporate employees, still less corporate bosses in a time of corporate production of food, but instead the keepers of place and memory.

They are the ones who stop on dusty lanes to ask, at once open and guarded, what my friends and I are up to with our cameras, notebooks, birding handbooks, and out-of-state license plates. We are allies, we discover, but we do not live here. They do, and in the battle to protect their land, which they fight every day, they are rightly the generals.

Their lives, their ways of life, are emphatically not things to be dashed by a bulldozer blade or scratched out by a bureaucrat's pen. There is certainly no room in this vision for derricks and highways, trucks and

39. The Guadalupe Mountains at sunset. Photograph by Stephen Capra.

stolen futures. The thieves and devourers hunger for it, but it is time for once to say no: no more national sacrifice areas, no more destruction for eons to satisfy ephemeral greed, no more fragmentation, no more Hobbesian politics, no more Band-Aid solutions to gaping wounds. No more decisions made about the American land by an administration that has ceded jurisdiction over it to millenarian antienvironmentalists of the James Watt school, that nakedly disdains the very notion of environmental protection and stewardship, that has approved the destruction of countless acres of the public domain in the name of Orwellian programs such as the "healthy forests" and "clean skies" initiatives, which, borrowing a page from the so-called Wise Use movement, mean exactly the opposite of what they say.

"Too often the Western states have been prosperous at the expense of their fragile environment," wrote the historian and novelist Wallace Stegner toward the end of his life, wondering whether the geography of hope—a term he coined—was really hopeless, as he feared it might be. "And their civilization has too often mined and degraded the natural scene while drawing most of its quality from it." The odds were long, he allowed, but even so, he concluded,

> Somehow, against probability, some sort of indigenous, recognizable culture has been growing on Western ranches and in Western towns and even in Western cities. It is the product not of the boomers but of the stickers, not of those who pillage and run but of those who settle and love the life they have made and the place they have made it in. I believe that eventually, perhaps within a generation or two, they will work out some sort of compromise between what must be done to earn a living and what must be done to restore health to the earth, air, and water.

40. Grass in seed, fall. Photograph by Stephen Strom.

It is far from the highway, far from the center of things, far from most people's thoughts. Even by the big-sky standards of the West, it is a remote place, all too easy to overlook. But Otero Mesa, this extraordinary, necessary place, is at a crossroads. Which vision of the future will direct its course? What way of life will it inform?

At Otero Mesa, we have the chance to say no—and in an entirely positive, hopeful way that looks toward a better future for the West and the world, repudiating the greed and short-sightedness of faraway carpetbaggers. The right path is obvious: not another highway, not another derrick, not another pipeline, but a rutted trail over stone and grass, honeycombed with burrows and lined with thorns, patrolled by pronghorns and diamondbacks and prairie dogs and a handful of humans, and always with an aplomado falcon watching from high above. ▪

41. An immature kestrel (*Falco sparverius*) in flight. Photograph by Stephen Strom.

Further Reading

Eve Ball. *Indeh: An Apache Odyssey*. Provo, UT: Brigham Young University Press, 1980.

Rick Bass. *Oil Notes*. Boston: Houghton Mifflin, 1989.

Rick Bass and Paul Christensen, eds. *Falling from Grace in Texas: A Literary Response to the Demise of Paradise*. San Antonio, TX: Wings Press, 2004.

Alan Boye. *Tales from the Journey of the Dead: Ten Thousand Years on an American Desert*. Lincoln: University of Nebraska Press, 2007.

Lauren Brown. *Grasslands*. New York: Knopf, 1985.

Álvar Núñez Cabeza de Vaca. *Adventures in the Unknown Interior of America*. Albuquerque: University of New Mexico Press, 1983.

Gerard J. DeGroot. *The Bomb: A Life*. Cambridge, MA: Harvard University Press, 2005.

Mark E. Eberhart. *Feeding the Fire: The Lost History and Uncertain Future of Mankind's Energy Addiction*. New York: Harmony Books, 2007.

Frederick R. Gehlbach. *Mountain Islands and Desert Seas: A Natural History of the U.S.-Mexican Borderlands*. College Station: Texas A&M University Press, 1981.

John Graves. *From a Limestone Ledge*. Dallas, TX: Southern Methodist University Press, 1980.

Jeffrey Greene. *Water from Stone: The Story of Selah, Bamberger Ranch Preserve*. College Station: Texas A&M University Press, 2007.

Norman J. Hyne. *Nontechnical Guide to Petroleum Geology, Exploration, Drilling and Production*. 2nd ed. Tulsa, OK: Penn Well, 2001.

Richard L. Knight, Wendell Gilgert, and Ed Marston, eds. *Ranching West of the 100th Meridian: Culture, Ecology, and Economics.* Washington, DC: Island Press, 2002.

Michael Kort. *The Columbia Guide to the Cold War.* New York: Columbia University Press, 1998.

Richard Manning. *Grassland: The History, Biology, Politics, and Promise of the American Prairie.* New York: Penguin, 1995.

Cormac McCarthy. *Cities of the Plain.* New York: Knopf, 1998.

Gregory McNamee. *Gila: The Life and Death of an American River.* New York: Crown, 1994.

Francis Moul. *The National Grasslands: A Guide to America's Undiscovered Treasures.* Lincoln: University of Nebraska Press, 2006.

Morris E. Opler. *Apache Odyssey: A Journey between Two Worlds.* New York: Holt Rinehart Winston, 1969.

Kevin Phillips. *American Theocracy: The Peril and Politics of Radical Religion, Oil, and Borrowed Money in the 21st Century.* New York: Viking, 2006.

Paul F. Starrs. *Let the Cowboy Ride: Cattle Ranching in the American West.* Baltimore, MD: Johns Hopkins University Press, 1998.

David J. Weber. *The Spanish Frontier in North America.* New Haven, CT: Yale University Press, 1992.

Matthew Yeomans. *Oil: Anatomy of an Industry.* New York: New Press, 2004.

Daniel Yergin. *The Prize: The Epic Quest for Oil, Money, and Power.* New York: Simon & Schuster, 1992.